water gardens

by Susan Lang, T. Jeff Williams, and the Editors of Sunset Books

Menlo Park, California

SUNSET BOOKS

VICE PRESIDENT, GENERAL MANAGER
Richard A. Smeby
VICE PRESIDENT, EDITORIAL DIRECTOR
Bob Doyle
PRODUCTION DIRECTOR
Lory Day
DIRECTOR OF OPERATIONS
Rosann Sutherland
RETAIL SALES DEVELOPMENT MANAGER
Linda Barker
EXECUTIVE EDITOR
Bridget Biscotti Bradley
ART DIRECTOR
Vasken Guiragossian

STAFF FOR THIS BOOK

MANAGING EDITOR
Barbara Ferguson Stremple
ART DIRECTORS
Alice Rogers, Deborah Cowder
SUNSET BOOKS SENIOR EDITOR
Sally W. Smith
WRITERS
Susan Lang, T. Jeff Williams
COPY EDITOR
Pamela Evans
ILLUSTRATORS
Rik Olson, Elisa Tanaka,
Tracy La Rue Hohn, Jenny Speckels
PREPRESS COORDINATOR
Danielle Javier
INDEXER
Nanette Cardon
PROOFREADER
Alicia K. Eckley

FRONT COVER PHOTOGRAPHY
Marcus Harpur

For additional copies of *Water Gardens* or any
other Sunset book, call 1-800-526-5111 or
visit us at *www.sunsetbooks.com*.

Water in the Garden

Of all the aspects of a garden, water is easily the most compelling and lyrical. Water adds a dimension distinct from those of plants, wildlife, statuary, and stone—yet it brings all of those elements together. You can add water to almost any space imaginable, whether you create a delightful spill fountain by your front door, a serene koi pond by the patio, a musical stream tumbling through the garden, or a grand waterfall cascading down a hilly part of your landscape.

Water has the capacity to energize in the spring, cool in the summer, soothe in the fall, and inspire in the winter. And gardens with water allow you to design an oasis of new types of plants that would not otherwise grow in your yard.

Beyond gardening, a pond allows you to tend fish, enjoy visiting birds, and delight in the frogs, dragonflies, and other creatures that seek out your special retreat.

In this book we have given you all the information necessary to create a fabulous water feature—covering topics from design to equipment, construction, planting, fishkeeping, and finally, maintenance. If you are like most water gardeners, you'll find that your initial project will be just that. As you near completion of this first endeavor, you will be eyeing other areas in the landscape that just might benefit from some type of water magic.

Special thanks are due to Bob Gordon of Pond Systems in Santa Rosa, California, for lending his expertise in the creation of this book.

contents

CHAPTER ONE

The Magic of Water Gardens

WHETHER IN THE FORM OF A RUSHING WATERFALL, a water lily pond, or a small bubbling fountain, a water garden can transform landscapes from the commonplace to the extraordinary. Water features make yards more alluring—for people as well as wildlife. Both benefit from water's magical ability to soothe and refresh. ❧ *There are no constraints on how you define a water garden—as long as there's water somewhere (even if it's only seasonal runoff down an otherwise dry creekbed). You can express yourself as you please, perhaps by incorporating whimsical elements or taking up fishkeeping. For inspiration, check out the many types of water gardens depicted in this chapter.* ❧ *After you install your water garden, you'll wonder how you ever got along without it. You'll also be the latest in a long line of people, dating back to early recorded history, who have happily fallen under waterscaping's spell.*

Why a Water Garden?

Water gardens offer so much more than just beauty—though they provide that in abundance. They're also havens of peace and tranquility, places in which to relax and commune with nature. This type of gardening is so satisfying that even seasoned water gardeners marvel at its addictive quality— the ongoing desire to dig another pond, work in a waterfall, extend a stream, add a fountain.

A REFUGE OF CALM

A well-conceived water garden serves as a sanctuary from daily cares. Check your worries at the back door or garden gate and enter a magical world of serene sights and sounds. Just what constitutes serenity depends on the individual, of course—for one it may be a still pool that reflects an azure sky or graceful plants waving in the breeze; for another it may be a thundering waterfall; for a third it may be a school of fish gliding gracefully among water lilies.

A calming waterscape can make you forget, if only temporarily, life's petty annoyances. These may include background noises of everyday life: the rumble of traffic, the distant beat of music, the persistent bounces of a basketball. The musical sounds of moving water—trickling, splashing, gurgling, bubbling, gushing —not only mask unwanted

Falls don't have to be big or booming. The subdued splashes of this small waterfall are soothing yet muffle many neighborhood noises. Fencing and heavy planting also buffer sounds from the street and add to the sense of privacy.

noises but are pleasing in themselves. These agreeable sounds have an almost tranquilizing effect, distracting your attention from unpleasant ones or actually drowning them out.

A TRUE OASIS

If you live in an arid or hot climate, you'll find that a water garden refreshes in another sense: it's a spot of lush, liquid relief in an otherwise blistering environment, just like an oasis in a desert.

A pond or other water feature conveys coolness, regardless of the ambient temperature. The effect may be largely psychological, but if you feel cool and refreshed, who's to argue?

A WILDLIFE HAVEN

A water garden is as much an oasis for animals as for humans. It attracts many kinds of wildlife, including songbirds, turtles, and amphibians such as frogs.

Of course you can also stock your waterway with ornamental fish like colorful koi and goldfish—they will add vitality and movement, even personality, to the garden.

If you do keep fish, you may have to contend with occasional unwelcome wildlife, like raccoons and herons. However, most water gardeners feel that the desirable guests more than make up for having to thwart a few pesky callers.

EXPANDED HORIZONS

If you're already an enthusiastic "land gardener," you'll enjoy the challenge of learning a different kind of gardening. Your yard may already be filled with diverse plantings, but as a water gardener you can cultivate new and interesting plants that won't grow on dry land, such as water lilies and other floating plants.

And as a water gardener, you're not limited to plants. The opportunity to learn about fishkeeping—especially if you've never kept so much as a single goldfish in a glass bowl—can be extremely satisfying.

ABOVE: *A streamside deck is the perfect place to enjoy the cooling effects of this lush water garden. Even if the water doesn't actually lower the temperature (although it may seem to), the palm trees and other tropical plantings will keep loungers comfortable by shading the deck.*

BELOW: *A water garden can be a refuge for many kinds of wildlife. Goldfish and koi were introduced into this pond. Amphibians often show up on their own, as did this frog, pictured in the inset.*

Natural Beauty

Some water gardens look like authentic aspects of the natural landscape, whereas others may be designed to evoke nature rather than duplicate it in every detail.

▲ *A STEEP HILLSIDE is the ideal location for dramatic falls. Here, water rushes over a series of wide spill stones before plunging into a holding pool below.*

▲ *THIS INFORMAL POND in a woodsy setting includes a small, subtle waterfall that provides pleasing sounds yet doesn't disrupt the pond's overall glassy, calm surface.*

▶ *LOW-GROWING, NATURALISTIC PLANTINGS and abundant rocks contribute to the alpine spirit of these pools and connecting waterfalls that are constructed on hilly terrain.*

ARTISTICALLY ARRANGED
large boulders and slabs create the height needed for cascading waterfalls and stepped pools. Even if the country-side is miles away, these faux ducks suggest otherwise.

THIS MEANDERING GARDEN STREAM
in the Colorado Rockies features locally quarried rock and takes advantage of breathtaking natural vistas.

Personal Sanctuary

Many kinds of water gardens—with different features, styles, and settings—can be havens from everyday concerns. Anything goes, as long as it's your idea of sanctuary.

◀ ***THIS PLANT LOVER'S WATER GARDEN*** *consists of a spill fountain— a stream of water pouring from one barrel into another— barely concealed by a luxuriant, tropical-looking planting.*

▲ ***THE DECK IS A REFUGE*** *from which to enjoy the movement and sounds of water running in the stream below. Dense plantings on the banks are an additional feast for the eyes.*

▼ **THIS VISUALLY REFRESHING** water feature is fitting for someone whose taste runs to the formal: a circular fish pond and urn-shaped fountain neatly anchor a landscape based on geometric shapes and symmetry.

▲ **CHEERY SEASONAL COLOR** borders the stacked rock slabs forming this multilevel pool located near a home's entrance. When you're in the house, sanctuary is a quick escape away.

THE BENCH by this raised concrete pool at the far edge of a terrace is a quiet perch on which to think—or to simply enjoy the flowerlike sculpture in the corner of the pool.

Small and Simple

Good things often do come in small packages. Features like these could be the sole water display on a property, or they could supplement larger water gardens.

► ***THERE'S NOTHING SIMPLER*** *or more charming than a well-designed birdbath set amid colorful plantings like these spring bulbs.*

▼ ***TUCKED INTO A BORDER,*** *this small bowl fountain contains stones chosen for their bleached colors and interesting shapes. The slight trickle of water over the bowl's edges is enough to capture the attention of passersby.*

► **A TUB GARDEN** brings the delights of water gardening closer to eye level. Even a fairly small decorative pot can hold several kinds of aquatic plants and a few small fish.

▲ **A BEAUTIFUL CONTAINER** like this shimmering aqua-colored pot can be filled with water, planted with aquatic species, or turned into a fountain.

▲ **IN THIS RUSTIC FOUNTAIN,** water flows down a hollowed post into a stone trough. The trickling sound is gentle yet persistent enough to be heard throughout a small garden.

IN A MILLSTONE FOUNTAIN, water bubbles up from the center and flows down grooves in the stone. The fountain is set in the embrace of a large planting of hostas, which visually softens the edges of the stone.

Artistic License

Water gardens offer wonderful opportunities to be creative or whimsical and to show your artistic side. Placing art in the setting also adds drama and interest.

WHY HAVE AN ORDINARY BIRDBATH when beautiful, stylized shapes are available? This birdbath may remind one person of a toadstool with an indented cap, or another person of an open flower.

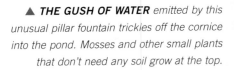

▲ **THE GUSH OF WATER** emitted by this unusual pillar fountain trickles off the cornice into the pond. Mosses and other small plants that don't need any soil grow at the top.

▶ **IN THIS DROLL FOUNTAIN,** water bubbles out of the top of the umbrella and cascades down its sides into the pool. Meanwhile, the bronze woman remains dry —only the bottoms of her feet appear to be touching the water's surface.

▲ **WATER SPILLS** *from multiple outlets in this stone wall into the raised pool below. In a whimsical touch, a school of metallic fish swims merrily along the wall.*

◄ **WATER IS OFTEN USED** *for its reflective quality. Here, a little curlicued birdbath contains not just water but also a gazing ball, doubling the reflections.*

FOUNTAINS ARE AVAILABLE *in many fanciful forms—and what could be more appropriate for a garden pond than a fish motif? Here, water streams from the fish's mouth into the pond.*

The trough pool and dish fountain pictured here are at the heart of just one of many magnificent water gardens at the Alhambra Palace in Spain. The builders were innovative in their use of water, which they used to cool the palace grounds, reflect the beautiful surroundings, and create musical sounds.

Water Gardens through the Ages

From ancient Egypt to modern-day America, virtually every culture and every age has adopted the practice of water gardening, altering and refining it to suit their own philosophies and practical needs.

AN ANCIENT TRADITION

The early civilizations of Egypt and Mesopotamia first harnessed water into channels for irrigation and to protect themselves from flooding. Gradually, they began to use water decoratively, adding fish and plants to beautify the channels. Illustrations on Egyptian tombs dating back to 3000 B.C. show gardeners tending lotuses.

Water was at the heart of gardens in ancient Persia, where the "fourfold" garden, a geometric design with strong religious symbolism, developed. It consisted of a walled square divided into four equal parts by two canals, with a pool in the center. The design survived Persia's fall to Macedonia in the fourth century B.C., outlasted the Roman invasion 300 years later, and endured through the invasion by Muslim Arabs in A.D. 642. The Muslims embraced the design and carried it with them across the Mediterranean region as far west as Spain, where superb examples can still be seen at the Alhambra Palace above Granada. In these hot regions, water gardens were valued for their cooling effects.

To the east, the Mongol leader Genghis Khan carried Islamic traditions to India in the 16th century. The exquisite reflecting pools at the Taj Mahal stand today as a reminder of that legacy.

The ancient Romans applied their profound knowledge of hydraulics gained from building networks of aqueducts to create elaborate water gardens featuring baths, pools, canals, waterfalls, fountains, and statues of deities. They exported their style throughout Europe, North Africa, and Asia.

DAZZLING DISPLAYS

At a standstill in Europe during the Dark Ages, the practice of water gardening experienced a revival in the Renaissance. In Italy, garden planners took hydraulics to the nth degree, leaving the extravagant displays at Villa d'Este and elsewhere as testaments to their ingenuity. Their innovation was to create dramatic movements of water, sending it gushing into the air or cascading down hilly terrain. They also used water in jest—for example, slyly concealing water jets that would then be triggered by any unsuspecting passersby. (Contemporary water gardeners who create lily ponds in bathtubs set outdoors or demonstrate drollery in other ways are therefore following a well-established tradition.)

France borrowed many of the ornate aspects of Italian water gardens but applied them in a strictly formal, geometric manner. In the 17th century, upon moving his court to Versailles, Louis XIV built extravagant gardens featuring more than 10,000 water jets. Unfortunately, not enough water could be pumped fast enough to operate them simultaneously, so the king settled for running them in sequence as he guided visitors through the royal gardens.

NATURALISM

Much earlier, the Chinese had established a tradition of natural-ism, reflecting their belief that one way to enlightenment was through communion with nature. By including artistic representations of ponds, lakes, and other water features in their gardens, they created peaceful places in which to contemplate nature.

The Japanese later refined the Chinese approach to water gardening, infusing it with detailed symbolism and simplifying the elements. They were also the first to breed colorful varieties of the carp, or koi, that still inhabit our garden ponds.

In the 18th century, long after the Asians had mastered naturalism, Europe began to experiment with less formal water garden styles. After finding the geometric French style unsuited to their more hilly landscape, the English in particular became known for naturalistic water gardens whose focus was the water itself.

MODERN WATER GARDENS

In the 19th century, English garden makers moved the spotlight to plants, as explorers sent home huge numbers of new species. Monet's water lily-filled garden at Giverny in France serves as a benchmark in the shift to plants as the focus of interest in water gardens.

Monet's painterly approach gained favor in the 20th century. On this continent, designers gave it a North American stamp, adapting it to our diverse regions and scaling it down to fit smaller spaces. No longer were water gardens solely the province of landscape architects designing for wealthy clients.

The advent of liners and other products made water gardens accessible to ordinary people. Now anyone with even a modest patch of land can enjoy the pleasures of a water garden.

The grand Belgian estate Annevoie contains more than 20 ornamental ponds and lakes fed by dozens of water jets and falls. The displays have gushed, spewed, and sprayed water continuously for more than 250 years.

CHAPTER TWO

Planning and Design

ANY PROPERTY, from a postage stamp–size urban lot to a large country estate, can accommodate a water garden. It doesn't matter whether the land is level or hilly; the water may come from a municipal supply, a well, or some other source. It doesn't matter if your budget is large or small. Regardless of circumstances, there is a way to feature water in every landscape and some arrangement that will work for every aspiring water gardener. This chapter will help you choose a suitable site in your yard and decide on a general type of water garden, as well as a size and style. You'll find advice for putting your plans on paper and for budgeting and timing the work. And—if you decide you can't handle the entire project yourself—you'll learn how to get help from experts.

The Right Site

Look for a place that's fairly sunny, fairly level (unless you want a waterfall), and fairly close to water and electricity sources. Just as important, find a spot that will allow you to easily view and enjoy your water garden, and one where the water will reflect the beautiful surroundings.

SUNLIGHT

For good bloom on water plants, the site should get 5 or 6 hours of direct sunlight daily. Most water lilies and other blooming aquatic plants will put on a good show in such a spot, yet there will still be enough shade to deter excess algae growth. In the hottest climates, avoid the most intensely sunny locations; the water can get too hot, and it will evaporate very quickly.

In a very shady yard, you may be able to thin out trees and large shrubs to allow in more light. If sunlight is still sparse but you do want some plants, find the sunniest spot and choose shade-tolerant ones (consult the plant encyclopedia beginning on page 136).

When judging the amount of light your proposed site gets, remember that sun and shade patterns change throughout the year; shadows are shorter in summer, when the sun is higher in the sky. Also, a site that's sunny in early spring may be shady by summer, after deciduous trees have leafed out and perennials have gained height.

You might think that a koi pond, which typically contains little or no aquatic plant life to shade the water, should be located out of direct sunlight, but the fish actually do well in full sun. Although sun-warmed water contains less oxygen than the cooler water of semishade, that won't be a problem if the pond is deep enough (see "Home, Sweet Home" on page 157) and has a pump for aeration.

WIND

Gentle breezes are fine, but prevailing winds and gusts can blow spray from a fountain every which way and cause water to evaporate quickly.

If your best site gets too much wind, consider creating a windbreak. An impenetrable barrier like a solid fence may seem like a good idea, but the wind will rise up over it and come down on the other side with greater force. A hedge or lattice fence, with gaps that allow some air through to diffuse the wind, is a better choice.

TERRAIN

You could spend a lot of money and regrade your land to accommodate a water feature that doesn't logically belong there

LEFT: *The best kind of windbreak is one that lets some wind pass through, such as the lattice and rail fences shown here. As wind filters through all the fence openings, it loses force.*

FACING PAGE, TOP: *Waterfalls look natural cascading down hillsides. On this property, the falls are located near the house, following a channel formed by rain runoff.*

(such as a waterfall on a perfectly flat lot), but it makes more sense to take advantage of your property's natural contours. A steep slope is an ideal site for dramatic falls; a flat lot, for a still pool.

It's easiest to build pools and other water basins on fairly level land. But if you must work with a slope, you can terrace the area where the pond will be built (see page 54).

Be careful if you select the base of a slope or another low spot for a pond; it will not only become a frost pocket but may also be flooded by rainwater runoff. You'll have to solve the problem of potential flooding by building up the perimeter to redirect the surface runoff and installing a drainage system to divert excess underground water.

Identify any water, sewer, gas, electrical, telephone, or other buried utility lines in your yard so that you can avoid digging in those areas. (See "Call Before You Dig" on page 50.) Another potential impediment is a high water table, which can damage a pool and cause the liner to float. To determine if your water table is high, dig a hole to the pool's proposed depth and let it stand open during the wettest time of year. If the hole fills with water on a rainless day, the water table there is too high. If this is true throughout the yard, you may have to opt for a raised pool, fountain, or a tub garden.

Finally, be sure to consider where water will drain when you clean the pool or when it overflows. If the only natural drainage is onto your neighbor's property or under your house, you'll need to install a man-made drain of some kind.

Existing Landscape?

Finding room for a small accent like a birdbath or a tub garden is easy, even in a densely planted garden. But a more prominent feature like a water lily pond deserves careful siting. Rather than shoehorn it into the first available spot, decide which site would work best—even if something else is already there. It's better to spend the extra time booting out the current resident of that space, whether shrubbery, lawn, or brick paving, than to settle for a poor site.

Before making a final decision, consider how much trenching through plantings and walkways is needed to bring water or electricity to your new water garden. You may want to rethink your site selection if you have to dig up too much of the garden. Or perhaps you would be just as happy with a different kind of water feature—for example, a still pool that you can fill by hose rather than one requiring a pump and water pipes.

TREES

The idea of nestling a pond under a tree or large shrub may appeal to you, but remember that such a spot is often too shady for most water plants to thrive. Also, fallen leaves and other plant debris will rot at the bottom of the pond, creating water quality problems—you can skim a lot of material out of the water, but it's hard to retrieve the small particles. A fountain might be a better way to bring water to a shady spot. It's easy to scoop leaves out of a fountain, and no fish or plants will suffer if the water quality is occasionally poor.

To minimize leaf debris, avoid siting your pond directly below overhanging limbs—and, if possible, locate it beyond a nearby tree's dripline (the outside edge of the tree canopy). Keep it even farther away from trees with invasive roots, such as willows and poplars.

You can cut into a few tree roots when you dig, but severing too many or very large ones may harm the tree. If the spot you're considering is dense with roots, look for another site.

POINT OF VIEW

Position your water garden for your own maximum enjoyment, where you can readily see and—in the case of moving water—hear it.

For many people, the ideal spot is near a deck or patio. You may concur if you live in a climate where you can relax outdoors much of the year.

But if typically rainy or chilly weather reduces the time you spend outdoors, consider a site you can view from a frequently used room indoors.

On the other hand, you may prefer a site along a well-traveled garden path. Or you can tuck the water garden into a corner of the yard, to create a secluded place for quiet meditation.

This charming cherub birdbath is a good choice for a shaded, leafy spot. In addition to brightening the area, it attracts birds to the garden. Also, fallen leaves are easy to remove from the water.

ABOVE: *A seating area adjoining the house is the ideal spot for a garden featuring moving water. Even if you're indoors, the musical sounds can be heard through open windows.*

LEFT: *A bricked porthole provides a perfectly framed view of a formal water garden.*

WATER AND POWER

It makes sense to build your water feature within a reasonable distance of your water source if you plan to lay pipe connecting the two. Having a hose bib nearby will facilitate filling and topping off the pond. For information on various types of water sources, see below.

Proximity to an electrical hookup is also handy if you need power to run a pump or filter. The easiest solution is to plug into an existing outlet—either an outdoor one on the deck or exterior house wall, or an indoor one in the garage or toolshed. If you use low-voltage equipment (see page 78) it's easy to run the cord to your water feature. In a sunny climate you can opt for solar-powered equipment, to avoid hooking into your home's electrical system. But unless you're powering a water feature that runs only during the daytime, you'll need batteries and a transformer to keep the equipment going at night.

Water Sources

Consider the source before you start building, so you'll be ready to address any water quality problems. Quantity shouldn't be a problem—you need a large amount of water for the first fill only; thereafter, the pool will require just modest topping off.

MUNICIPAL WATER

If you live in an urban or suburban area, you probably draw from a municipal water supply that has been treated with chlorine or chloramine (a combination of ammonia and chlorine). Both are toxic to fish but chlorine will break down if exposed to the air. Chlorine and chloramine —which doesn't break down—can easily be treated. See "Harmful Chemicals" on page 165.

WELL WATER

If you live in the countryside, you probably get your water from a well. You can have the water tested to find out if it contains anything that may adversely affect plants or fish.

Unless your system is hooked up to a chlorinator, the water is not likely to be chemically treated. But water from a well is often hard (that is, contains excess minerals); it won't harm plants or fish, but it may clog plumbing. High levels of iron can rust pools; well owners with iron problems often have holding tanks where the iron can settle out. Well water can also be too acidic for plant and fish health; see page 179 for information about adjusting the pH level.

NATURE'S BOUNTY

If there's a natural spring, creek, or stream on your property that flows year-round, it could be a good source for your water garden—though you may need permission from the proper authorities to tap in.

The water may look pristine, but be sure to check it regularly: there's no way to know what someone upstream may be dumping into it. Also, the water may be a little too cold for plants and fish; diverting it into a shallow holding pool on its way to your water garden will warm it up.

Wet Areas

Rather than construct a feature like a fountain or pond and fill it with water, you may want to turn a naturally wet area (even if it's only seasonally wet) into a water garden. Or you could do both—build from scratch in one area and take advantage of nature in another.

BOG GARDENS

A constantly damp area is ideally suited to plants that appreciate plentiful moisture. Just be sure that the soggy soil is due to a natural cause—like a high water table or rainwater runoff— rather than to a broken pipe or malfunctioning septic system.

It's best to line the bog with pond liner. This defines the area and allows you to keep the soil uniformly moist. Dig out the area to about 14 inches deep, then lay the liner (hiding the edges for appearance's sake) and poke some holes in the material with a garden fork. Cover the liner with a 2-inch layer of pea gravel and return the soil to the hole.

A bog can be a breeding ground for mosquitos when it contains standing water, but careful preparations will facilitate its drainage. If water does accumulate in warm weather, you can direct the surplus away. (In cold weather, mosquitos are inactive.)

If the boggy spot dries out during periods of drought, either

A bog garden occupies the naturally moist ground that flanks a narrow stream running through this backyard. The plants chosen for this garden grow best with constant moisture.

choose moisture-loving plants that can endure some dryness or be prepared to water the bog on occasion.

RAIN GARDENS

In some locales with regular summer rainfall, homeowners are being encouraged to plant "rain" gardens in sites where rainwater (or snow melt) collects. The idea is to direct runoff from roofs, gutters, driveways, and landscape surfaces—and the pollutants that they contain—away from

sewers, thus decreasing the amount of water that municipalities must treat.

Rain gardens typically consist of a saucerlike depression, dug only about a foot deep in the middle, where the runoff collects. Most rain gardeners mix materials like mulch and gravel in the saucer to improve the drainage. The lowest area, in the middle of the depression, is reserved for plants that like truly boggy conditions but can tolerate occasional drying out. The inside perimeter of the saucer is suited to plants that thrive with moisture but can also take some drought. The driest area, surrounding the depression, is for a mix of regionally adapted plants. Check with your water district for lists of suitable plants.

An ideal location for a rain garden is near a downspout; attach a flexible drainpipe to the bottom of the downspout to direct rainwater runoff at least several feet away from the house. Another good spot is along the low edge of a driveway that slopes to one side.

DRY CREEKBEDS

These naturalistic features are especially popular in regions with dry summers. You line a channel with rocks, pebbles, and gravel to give the impression of a waterway—even when it's devoid of water. The secret lies in carefully arranging the stones to look as if the force of water had shaped the channel.

A dry creekbed laid on a long sloping path doubles as a drainage channel for seasonal runoff. You can locate it along natural depressions and troughs already formed by runoff, or start the creekbed at the open end of a drainage pipe. Unlike a constructed stream meant to hold water, a dry creekbed does not need a waterproof lining, since it will be dry most of the time. But plan to install a liner if you'd like water to be carried away to a drain. Instructions for making a dry creekbed are on pages 112–113.

NATURAL WATERWAYS AND WETLANDS

Incorporating your property's natural stream, creek, or wet lowland into your water garden design may seem like an obvious idea. However, contact your Cooperative Extension Office before you do anything to alter a natural body of water, even if the changes seem minor. Planting along the shore or introducing a few fish can have unforeseen consequences. And diverting water or changing contours may be strictly prohibited.

If the waterway or wetland is protected, then enjoy it in its natural state. Count yourself lucky to have such a scenic water feature—and one that nature has built for you.

ABOVE: *A natural creek on this property was the logical spot for a water garden. The homeowners planted the banks but were careful not to alter the course of the creek.*

LEFT: *In this dry creekbed, river rocks have been arranged in a sinuous path to evoke a natural stream.*

Water Safety

Take safety into account when planning a water garden, especially if you have young children. First, check local regulations to find out if you must provide certain safety features, such as a fence.

PROTECTING YOUNG CHILDREN

Curious youngsters are those most at risk around a pool or other body of water. Toddlers can drown in less than a foot of water. Always keep an eye on children whenever they're in a yard with a water feature.

If you're still worried about their safety, you could erect fencing with a childproof lock or another barrier such as a rock wall or dense planting all the way around the pool. Or you could install some type of protective device—various companies sell floating alarms, covers, metal grids, and other safety accessories.

If you feel those precautions would spoil the looks of the water garden, or that you'd still worry anyway, then defer your dreams of a large water feature until the kids are older. In the meantime, you can put in a safer feature, such as a pebble-filled fountain with no standing water.

PROTECTING OTHERS

People of any age can stumble into a pool if they can't see it, or if the surface on which they're standing or walking is unstable. Illuminate any pool located in an area where people might walk at night. To prevent slipping, make sure that a walkway next to the water provides good traction. Stones around the edge should easily support an adult's weight; use heavy rocks and partially bury them so they won't tip over even if someone leans over the edge. Steps leading across a larger pond must be stable and accommodate the largest

Older children may be fine around a very shallow stream like this, but toddlers should be monitored closely whenever they're outdoors in a yard containing any kind of water feature. Caution should always be exercised when kids play around pools and ponds.

LEFT: *This wrought-iron fence encircling the pool is decorative and also protects young children from falling into the water.*

BELOW: *The low stone wall not only helps prevent people from accidentally tumbling into the pond, but its wide cap also serves as a convenient seat from which to enjoy the pond's beauty.*

feet. Install railings on bridges spanning ponds and on pondside decks, even if they're low to the ground.

If anyone does fall in, a shelf around the inside perimeter or a gradual slope to a pebble beach will provide an easy way out of the water. This, however, is at odds with protecting fish from predators—that design calls for a straight-edged, deep pool or one where any shelf is filled with plants (see page 173). If your priority is fishkeeping, take other protective measures if you feel they're necessary.

If the water feature runs on electricity, make sure the power cord is safely covered, so that no one trips over it. And, of course, any outdoor outlet should be protected by a GFCI (ground fault circuit interrupter).

A spacious water feature can accommodate large schools of fish as well as sizable plants in the water and on the banks. It can even contain a rowboat and dock as this pond does.

MOVING OR STILL?

Whether in the form of a waterfall, fountain, or coursing stream, moving water introduces satisfying sounds to the garden. It also contains more oxygen, a boon for fish. Movement can range from the turbulence of a gushing waterfall to the gentleness of a bamboo pipe trickling water over stones. In all cases, you'll need a pump to move and recirculate the water.

Still water brings peace and calm to a garden; the smooth surface is also valued for its reflective qualities. Unless it contains koi, a still body of water

What Kind of Water Garden?

Do you long for a fountain or a stream? If your fantasy calls for a pool, will it just contain water, or will you add plants or fish—or both? If you're partial to moving water, how should it move—trickle, spray, gush, cascade?

TYPES OF WATER FEATURES

Your many options include reflecting pools, water lily ponds, fish ponds, tub gardens, wall fountains, freestanding fountains, decorative waterspouts, waterfalls, streams, and dry creekbeds. You can choose more than one feature, installing them in different parts of the yard, or combine several elements in a single feature—for example, two ponds joined by a stream that is interrupted by falls.

Don't discount a feature because you think it's not right for your space and budget. Most water features can be scaled to fit your needs. A waterfall can be big and bold, cascading down a rocky slope—or it can be a subtle element tucked into the corner of a small pool. A pond can be big enough to row across, or small enough to reach from one side to the other. A stream can be a sizable body of water or a slender rivulet.

For a site at some distance from the house, you may want a birdbath or other simple water feature that doesn't require any plumbing or electricity. Building codes may govern the feature you have in mind (see page 41). If they are burdensome, you may decide in favor of a feature that poses no legal issues.

This simple Japanese-style fountain consists of a bamboo spout spilling water into a bowl. Rocks can be added to the bowl if desired.

probably won't need a filter. Water lilies and other plants grow best—and are better viewed—in still water.

You can enjoy the best of both worlds if your water garden is large enough to have movement in one part and stillness in another.

SUNKEN OR RAISED?

Pools can be set into the ground or raised completely or partially above it. A sunken body of water looks more natural than a raised one. However, you can feed and view fish much more easily in a raised pool.

Since a fully raised pool only requires excavation for the wall footings, it can be a good choice in a yard with very rocky or compacted soil. A raised structure is also a clever way to add some height to a flat landscape. Capping the edge provides pleasant seating and brings the feature closer to eye level.

WHAT'S IN THERE?

Will you be satisfied with just water—or do you want to add further beauty and interest in the form of plants and fish or other wildlife? To learn how plants and fish affect the ecological balance of a pond, see "The Nitrogen Cycle" on page 164.

PLANTS Different kinds of aquatic plants require different depths. Because of this, many water gardeners build a shelf around the

This pond packs a lot of appeal into a moderate-size space. Mass plantings are a feast for the eyes, while small falls provide a musical element as well as extra oxygen for the fish.

inside perimeter of the pond. A 10-inch width is common, but some gardeners prefer up to 24 inches wide, to accommodate large pots. The shelf can be a single depth or of varying depths (about 10 inches and 18 inches below the water line are popular choices). Plants generally do not grow well in splashing water, so keep them away from a waterfall or fountain. See the chapter beginning on page 114 for more about aquatic plants.

FISH The pool depth must be suitable for the type of fish you will keep; read about koi and goldfish requirements on pages 156–162. Fish need pollution-free, oxygenated water; depending on the type and number of fish, you may need a pump or a filter, or both. Koi are often kept in ponds with few or no

plants, since they shred vegetation and use their snouts to dig up roots.

The best way to protect fish from predators like raccoons and herons is to design a deep pond with straight sides and no easy access in or out of the water.

OTHER WILDLIFE If you don't have valuable fish to protect, you can design a pond that is inviting to other wildlife such as birds, turtles, and frogs—one that gives them easy access to the water. If you plan on a pebble beach at one side to encourage wading, allow enough space for a gradual slope into the water.

Style

Once you've decided on the elements of your water garden—perhaps a pool with plants and fish or a fountain with bubbling water—consider what you want the finished garden to look like.

CHOICES, CHOICES

You have many options when planning your water garden, just as you do when planning any other kind of garden. You may emphasize "hardscape"—hard surfaces like pools, fountains, and paving—and use plants as mere accents. On the other hand, you may give top billing to plants, both in the water and surrounding the pond. Or the object of your interest may be a collection of colorful koi.

Some water gardens have recognizable themes, such as the Japanese style. Others reflect a region's climate, as with a dry creekbed in the Southwest or a tropical garden in southern Florida. Still other water gardens are attuned to their immediate surroundings—for example, a stream running through a woodsy lot. If none of these choices seems quite right, you can opt for something that reflects your personal taste. You may even prefer a work of art—perhaps a fountain with water spilling through a series of unusual or homemade spill pans.

Some water garden styles are particularly suited to a formal landscape and others to a more naturalistic one, though it's often possible to blend the two approaches. Decide which style you find the most appealing.

FORMAL Strict formality is characterized by straight or geometric lines and symmetry. Generally, less space is devoted to plants than in an informal water garden. What plants there are usually have neat shapes, either because they grow that way or because they have been carefully pruned or trained.

A formal water feature looks as if it has been imposed on the landscape, rather than appearing there naturally. Often the pool or other feature is carefully located to be a focal point; it

In this formal garden, geranium-filled terra-cotta pots are placed symmetrically around the pool.

This informal garden features a meandering stream and waterfalls cascading into a small pond. Natural-looking plantings blanket the banks and spill into the water.

Informal pools are often rimmed with varied, irregular rocks and lush plantings that soften or even camouflage the edges.

COMPATIBILITY COUNTS

Be sure that the style you choose is compatible with other elements—for instance, the house, if it's within view of your water garden. Also consider the style of the rest of your yard, unless you're installing a landscape from scratch. If you're inserting your new water garden among formal beds and walkways, make it formal, too. If the surroundings are informal, on the other hand, treat the water garden similarly.

may line up with other prominent elements along a visual axis.

Formal pools can be raised, semi-raised, or sunken. Typical shapes are circles, ovals, squares, rectangles, and hexagons. Usually, the paving material around the pool is regularly sized and evenly spaced; brick and tile are common choices.

INFORMAL An informal, or naturalistic, water garden is characterized by flowing lines and curves, by a lack of symmetry, and by natural-looking plant forms. It

should appear to be an organic part of your landscape—or at least evocative of nature. For example, a stream should look as if its path has been cut by nature, perhaps with the beginning and end hidden to suggest a longer, meandering waterway. A small bubble fountain—water bubbling over stones—may bring to mind a natural spring.

Informal pools are usually sunken, their shape freeform or uneven. Some shapes may approach geometric ones but, as in nature, only imperfectly.

KOI POND SHAPES

Although many configurations are possible, koi ponds often have curved rather than angular corners. The shape—oval and kidney are popular choices—has less to do with style than with providing a good swimming environment for these active fish. Curves mean no obstacles or dead ends to slow them down. Also avoid sharp-edged rocks that could injure koi when they scrape against them.

Since this pool is small and shallow, the water in it will heat up quickly in warm weather and cool off rapidly when air temperatures drop.

Size

Think carefully about the dimensions of your water garden. If you're keen on having a pond, anything from a little tub garden to a lagoon-size reservoir will fit the bill, but choose a size that works for you. Also decide on the appropriate water depth and learn how to calculate the water volume.

OVERALL CONSIDERATIONS

You can go for big, small, or anything in between—it all depends on your desires, budget, and available space. If the water feature is mainly an accent, size it to suit the surroundings. But if it is a focal point, it should be large enough to be noticed.

You may want to make your pond a little larger than you'd planned, because it will look smaller when rocks and plants are added. Pond size is usually judged by the volume of water it contains: small ponds hold less than 500 gallons, medium-size ones 500 to 2,000, and large ones more than 2,000 (see pages 36–37 for how to figure water volume). Keep in mind that expanding in the future will be far more expensive and time-consuming than starting off bigger.

When determining the size of your water garden, don't forget the space requirements of any external equipment, such as a recirculating pump. Also allow space for any benches, paths, and transitional plantings that will connect the water feature to the adjoining landscape.

To clarify your thinking, it will help to inspect water gardens that friends or neighbors have, or those displayed at aquatic plant nurseries and public gardens. When you find one that seems close to the right size for the space you've chosen, measure it (including the depth). Don't just "eyeball" the size: it's easy to underestimate the dimensions.

You might think that larger ponds are more time-consuming to maintain than smaller ones, but the reverse is often true. One reason may be that every aspect of a small pond seems to be more noticeable. Whatever size of pond you settle on, if you don't want to do the upkeep, plan to hire someone experienced with water gardens to look after it. Many installers also offer a maintenance service.

WATER DEPTH

A water-only ornamental pool can be any depth you please—but if it's too shallow, it will look like a puddle (though dark stones blanketing the bottom can provide the illusion of depth). Also, excessive algae may pose a problem in a shallow pool. Depth is more critical when the pool contains fish or plants. The water should be deep enough to accommodate them comfortably and to avoid temperature fluctuations that may harm them.

The following depth guidelines are just that. Local pond owners and water garden suppliers can offer advice on ideal pool depths for your climate.

FOR FISH Generally, the colder your winters and the bigger your fish, the deeper the water should be. Deep water is also advisable in areas with very hot summers.

A fish pond should be deep enough to moderate temperature extremes, be they daily fluctuations (warm days and cool nights) or seasonal ones (hot summers and freezing winters). Deeper water also offers fish a refuge from predators. Depths of 2 to 3 feet are ideal in mild-winter climates; 3 to 4 feet in colder ones.

FOR PLANTS Each type of aquatic plant needs a specific depth (see the chapter beginning on page 114). Some water gardeners therefore build ponds with several depths, but others just prop up potted plants on supports to get them to the right level. Still others incorporate perimeter shelves to hold marginal plants (species that grow in water at the edges of a pond).

FOR AESTHETICS Looks are also a factor in determining the depth of a pool containing fish or plants. The greater the surface area, the deeper the water should be, to maintain pleasing proportions. A depth of 1½ feet is often recommended for small ponds with a surface area of up to 50 square feet. Increase the depth to 2 feet in ponds with a surface of up to 300 square feet, and to 2½ feet beyond that. (If fish or overwintering plants need even greater water depths for protection from freezing in your climate, be sure to add that to your figure.)

How Deep?

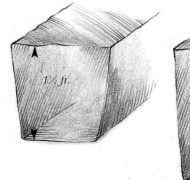

1½ ft.

Minimum depth for a pool containing plants or small fish in mild climates (ponds this shallow may freeze solid in wintry climates)

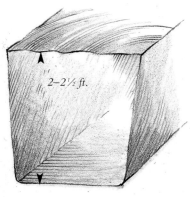

2–2½ ft.

Minimum depth for a pool in cold climates if you want to overwinter plants

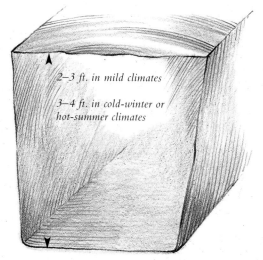

2–3 ft. in mild climates

3–4 ft. in cold-winter or hot-summer climates

Minimum depth for raising koi

Although it's possible to calculate the volume of an irregularly-shaped pond like this by adding up its dimensions, using the fill method below may be easier.

WATER VOLUME

Why do you need to know how many gallons of water your pool holds? For one thing, it tells you how many fish you can fit in the pool. It's also important when choosing a pump or filter, and when calculating how much salt or other remedy to add to the pool to dose your fish. Here are two methods of figuring your water volume.

FORMULAS To calculate the volume in gallons, multiply the surface area of the pool by your average depth times a conversion factor of 7.5 (roughly the number of gallons in a cubic foot of water). The examples of pools illustrated on the facing page assume straight sides and flat bottoms.

Since you need to know the surface area in order to complete the math, here's how to figure out the area of the various pool shapes:

- Rectangular or square: multiply length by width.
- Circular: multiply ½ diameter by ½ diameter by 3.14.
- Oval: multiply length by width by .80 (This assumes that the oval occupies about 80 percent of the space of a rectangle or square; multiply by .85 if the shape fills up more of the corners and by .75 if it eliminates more of the corners.)
- Odd shape: multiply average length by average width.

FILL IT UP Instead of using math to calculate water volume, you can simply gauge the amount of water that goes into the pool on its first fill-up.

- If you have a water meter, make sure water isn't running anywhere else on the property or in the house, then take a reading before the fill-up starts and again when it's finished—that's the number of gallons in the pool.
- If you're filling the pool by hose, time the number of minutes it takes. Then measure the time to fill a known capacity, such as a 5-gallon bucket. (Use the same hose, and turn the faucet on as far as it was turned before.) If the bucket fills in 25 seconds, the flow rate is 12 gallons per minute— 60 (seconds) divided by 25 (seconds to fill 5 gallons) multiplied by 5 (gallons in the bucket). If the pool takes 52 minutes to fill, it contains 624 gallons (52 times 12).
- For water piped into the pool, use the method described above for filling by hose. To figure out the flow rate, stick a bucket under the inlet valve feeding water into the pool.

KOI CAPACITY

Koi are big, active fish that need a lot of room. Figure on 300 gallons (large enough for three koi; see page 166) as the minimum size for a koi pond in mild-winter areas—for example, one roughly 4 feet wide by 6 feet long by 2 feet deep. In severe-winter areas, a koi pond should contain at least 600 gallons: the same length and width as the mild-winter pond, but 4 feet deep. This will be large enough for six koi.

How Much Water?

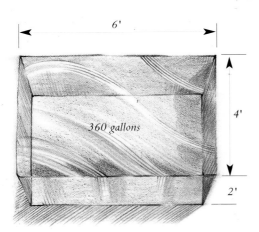

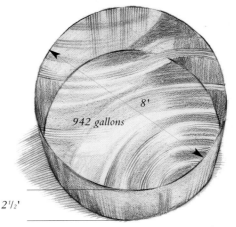

RECTANGULAR OR SQUARE POOL
length × width × average depth × 7.5
6' × 4' × 2' × 7.5 = 360 gallons
(surface area = 24 square feet)

CIRCULAR POOL
surface area × average depth × 7.5
50.24' × 2½' × 7.5 = 942 gallons
(surface area = 50.24 square feet)

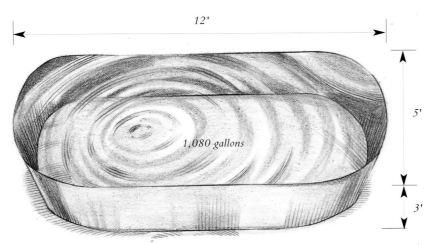

OVAL POOL
surface area × average depth × 7.5
48' × 3' × 7.5 = 1,080 gallons
(surface area = 48 square feet)

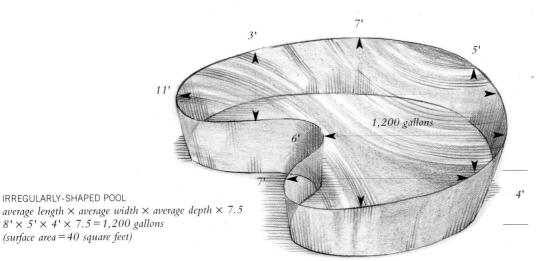

IRREGULARLY-SHAPED POOL
average length × average width × average depth × 7.5
8' × 5' × 4' × 7.5 = 1,200 gallons
(surface area = 40 square feet)

Making Plans

Once you've decided on the general location, type, and size of your water garden, draw a plan. It's better to clarify your ideas and work out any problems on paper rather than in the yard as you're digging. There's no need for a complex drawing—even a simple sketch, if carefully thought out, can serve as a reliable road map for installation. If you expect the plans to need approval by your building department, you'll have to draw a more precise diagram.

START DRAWING

Take accurate measurements of your site, then draw it to scale using graph paper or an architect's rule. Pencil in existing structures and landscape elements that you intend to keep, such as shrubs or planting beds. Mark underground utilities plus any hose bibs and electrical outlets in the vicinity. Also indicate which way the water drains; if you put your water garden in the path of runoff, you may have to divert it around the site.

Sketch in the pond or other water garden feature, trying various shapes, sizes, and positions until you find a combination you like. Mark the location of an external pump if you're using one. Draw in any structural or landscaping elements, including lights, that you'll be adding around the water feature.

DEVELOPING A PLAN

In this example of an odd-shaped lot, the moderate to steep slope in the backyard is the logical spot for a waterfall and stream, which could carry water to a pond where the land flattens out behind the house. You might want to incorporate a seating area at the top of the hill, so that you could enjoy a different perspective of the water garden than you'd get from the patio. To moderate the prevailing winds, you could plant more trees and tall shrubs along the northern and western property lines. Once you'd decided where major elements of the landscape would go, you could create a detailed planting plan for the water garden, transitional plants, and windbreak.

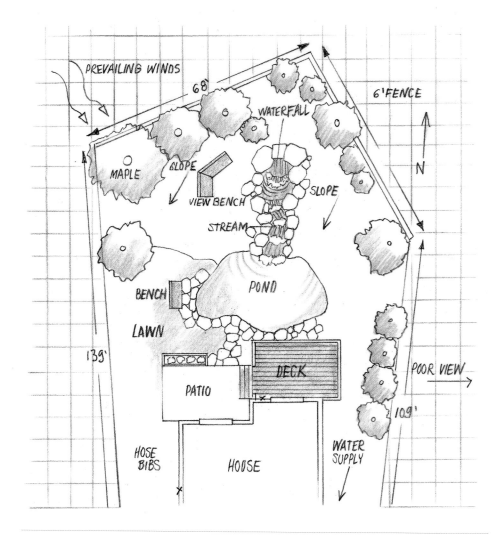

DON'T FORGET

Consider what to do with the soil you will be excavating (see page 40). You may want to integrate it into the design— perhaps by mounding it at one end to create a waterfall, or by building up the banks around the pond as planting beds. Or you may want to create berms or raised beds nearby. Sketch in possibilities on your plan to see what you like best.

Also consider how to handle the area immediately surrounding the pool. Lawn growing up to the edge can be attractive but is difficult to mow. Think about such options as boulders, paving, and plants. Since the water garden should be accessible for maintenance, include some way of getting to it that will work in both dry and wet weather—for example, stepping-stones or a gravel path.

TRY IT OUT

Outlining the water garden on the ground with rope, a garden hose, a trail of gypsum, or water-soluble spray paint will help you visualize it better. Adjust the outline until the location is just right and the proportions are pleasing.

Water gardens should reflect beautiful surroundings, so the dead tree mirrored in this pond will have to be removed. Consider what should be eliminated, or screened out, when you're planning your water feature.

Laying out related elements, such as a path leading to the feature, will give you a sense of the overall effect. Lay a mirror on the ground to get a good idea of what the water will reflect. If an eyesore shows up, reposition the body of water or add a screen—perhaps a trellis or tall plants—to your plan.

An Excavation Plan

To be sure the pool or other body of water has just the right contours and depths, make a sketch showing where and how much to dig. Also plan on paper before excavating a slope. With a little preparation, you'll have a better water garden while conserving your time and energy.

PUT IT ON PAPER

Show all parts of the water garden where digging is required, including the edging (perhaps for partially buried rocks) and any adjoining sitting area. Draw a band around each section that will be a different depth, such as marginal shelves, and indicate how deep it will be. It's also helpful to draw a cross section of the various depths, to help you visualize the work ahead.

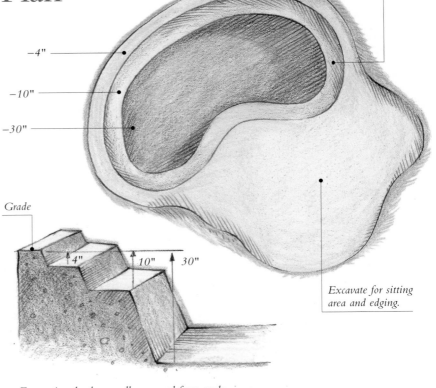

Excavate for marginal shelf.

−4"

−10"

−30"

Excavate for sitting area and edging.

Grade

4"   10"   30"

Excavation depths are all measured from grade.

Knowing how much to dig out of a hillside can be tricky, but a cross-sectional drawing will be helpful. The bottom of each boulder should be buried deeply enough to stabilize the rock, especially on steep slopes.

MOVING SOIL

Once you know the volume of your pond in gallons (see page 36), you can figure out just how much soil you'll have to excavate and move. You must move 1 cubic foot of soil to make room for 7½ gallons of water. For a small pool holding 450 gallons of water, that means excavating 60 cubic feet of soil. If you can move 4 cubic feet of soil at a time in your wheelbarrow, that's 15 wheelbarrow loads.

Do It Right

Check with your local building department to find out if there are any restrictions on your plans. Also let neighbors know your intensions so you can resolve any concerns they may have.

LEGALITIES

Local regulations may affect your water garden's design or add to the project's timeline and budget by requiring permits and inspections. Be scrupulously honest about what you're planning, so that you don't have any unpleasant surprises midway through installation.

In many areas, any pond more than 1½ feet deep requires a building permit. In certain locales, once the depth reaches 3 feet, a garden pond is classified as a swimming pool and is subject to a special permitting process. How deep the body of water is before it needs protective fencing varies from place to place, as does the height of a bridge before it needs a railing. You may also encounter restrictions that affect plumbing materials and electrical wiring.

Codes may govern how close to the property line you can build your water garden. You may even need a variance to put in the kind of water feature you want, and neighbors usually have the right to object to requests for variances. That's another good reason to discuss your plans with neighbors and be sure there are no objections from the start.

NEIGHBORS

Nearby residents may have qualms about certain aspects of your plans, such as the sound of a waterfall or the possibility of water spilling onto their property. Deal with their concerns in the planning stages. For example, change thundering falls to gentle cascades or incorporate a drainage system to handle runoff in locations that receive heavy rainfall. Conflicts are much more difficult and expensive to resolve once the water garden is in place.

If there are small children in the neighborhood, you may decide to include a fence (which may be required by law) or some other device to safeguard them. See "Water Safety" on pages 28–29.

DEALING WITH SLOPES

On uneven terrain, you'll have to create a level area for the water basin. You can do this by terracing the site and building a retaining wall (see "Terraces" and "Retaining Walls" on page 54).

On gentle inclines, a berm on the lower side can do the trick. In either case, contact your building department to determine that your plan is a safe one.

To create a berm, use the "cut and fill" technique: dig the water basin, then move the excavated soil to form a mound on the low side. Planting will help stabilize the relocated soil. Draw a cross section of the slope to help you plan the excavation; see the illustration below.

CREATING A BERM

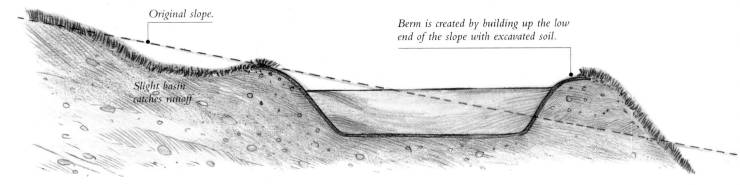

Original slope.

Berm is created by building up the low end of the slope with excavated soil.

Slight basin catches runoff

Hiring an Expert?

Planning and installing a pond or other water garden can be a lot of work, but there's no law that says you have to do everything yourself. You may want a professional to handle the entire project or simply help you with part of it.

EVALUATE YOUR NEEDS

If your project is simple—a tub garden, for instance—you can easily do it yourself. But you may appreciate some help with a larger and more complicated water garden, such as one con-

taining a waterfall. Be realistic about how much you can accomplish on your own, or with the help of family and friends.

Working with a professional isn't an all-or-nothing proposition. Perhaps you want someone to plan the garden, which you would then feel comfortable installing on your own. Or you may want to design it yourself and hire someone to do the labor. On the other hand, you may simply want to hand off the plumbing or electrical work. It's entirely up to you.

A complicated water garden like this—a pond with intersecting bridges built close to a house—is probably best left to a professional, unless you possess superior construction skills.

HIRE WITH CAUTION

Do a little research and, as the adage says, look before you leap.

- Find out who created the local water gardens that you admire. Check with water garden nurseries and suppliers in your area for recommendations— or they may offer design and installation services themselves. Groups like the American Society of Landscape

Architects or the Association of Professional Landscape Designers may also be able to suggest someone.

- Unless you're set on one highly recommended person, interview several candidates so that you can compare their work and job quotes. But don't call everyone in the business—that wastes their time and yours.

- Ask for references from former clients. Usually the professional will provide names of people who don't mind your viewing their garden. Arrange to visit the sites to inspect the work firsthand, and ask the clients whether the job was done on time and within budget.

- Although membership in a professional association doesn't guarantee quality, it does indicate a willingness to conform to rules and regulations and to submit to peer review. Some associations have a system for dealing with complaints from customers. Certain groups, like state landscape contractor associations, may tell you if any complaints have been filed against the person you're thinking of hiring.

- Don't make your decision on the basis of cost alone. Reputation and good personal communication can be just as important, or more so. Another factor to consider is how long you'll have to wait until your preferred professional is free to start the project.

- Professionals usually provide a contract; be sure to read it carefully and negotiate any changes before you sign it. To minimize the chance of misunderstandings later, the contract should spell out everything: the names of both you and the professional; the address where the work is to be done; the professional's responsibility for any accidents on the job site; specific descriptions of the materials and work involved; and an agreed-upon time schedule and payment plan. Both of you should sign the contract and keep a copy of it. You'll probably be asked to pay a deposit, but you shouldn't pay for any later phase of the project until it's satisfactorily completed.

A Roster of Experts

The following are some types of professionals who can help you. Additionally, specialty nurseries and water garden suppliers may offer design or installation services.

LANDSCAPE ARCHITECTS

Licensed by the state, landscape architects design and develop gardens. They can handle a project from concept through completion, producing detailed working plans, negotiating bids from subcontractors, and supervising the installation. If you don't want that much help, you can usually hire a landscape architect on an hourly basis for consultation or to produce a design.

LANDSCAPE DESIGNERS

This very general category encompasses a wide range of people with varying abilities; it's up to you to determine whether the people you interview are qualified to handle the work. Some offer the same services as landscape architects but aren't licensed, though they may be certified by a professional association.

LANDSCAPE CONTRACTORS

Most of these state-licensed professionals specialize in installing landscape elements such as ponds, paving, and plantings. Some are primarily designers who became licensed in order to be able to install their designs. Landscape contractors may do the actual work of putting in a garden, or they may hire subcontractors and oversee the project.

STRUCTURAL AND SOILS ENGINEERS

This type of expert is needed when a local building department requires an engineer's stamp on a project. Typically that happens when you're including a structure that will be built on a steep slope or on unstable soil.

Budgeting

Your budget will depend on the scope of the project and on whether you're hiring people to help you. Even if you plan to use a professional who will prepare a detailed budget, it doesn't hurt to run up some figures of your own.

BE METHODICAL

To develop a budget, first list the materials you need, such as a pond liner, pump, filter, and rocks. If you're not sure what's necessary, check the construction information and step-by-step projects in the chapters beginning on pages 46 and 72. Call or visit companies that sell water garden supplies and landscape materials to get rough costs.

KEEP IN MIND . . .

Here are some things to think about when budgeting.

- Use the best-quality materials you can afford.
- If there's poor access to the site, find out if there will be delivery surcharges.
- Prioritize your wishes and build in stages, if necessary.
- Focus on your goals. For instance, if you think you'll want more fish later on, a slightly more expensive, bigger pump is more cost-efficient than a smaller, cheaper one that you'll have to replace in a few years. The same goes for the size of the water garden itself: building bigger from the start is easier, and usually less expensive, than expanding at a later date.
- If your feature will have moving water or require filtration, you'll need the proper equipment and a source of power. The monthly cost of running pumps and filters can be substantial; talk to your water garden supplier or electric company for an estimate. Some water features can be turned off at will, but a biological filter must operate 24 hours a day.
- Consider the cost of a border and edging to be part of the basic cost of a pond. Accessory structures, such as a bench or a trellis, can be added in a later stage if you can't afford everything at once.
- Estimate the charges for equipment rentals (such as a backhoe for digging).
- Don't overlook the cost of fish and plants. This expense can vary greatly, depending on the types you select. With both fish and plants, however, you can start small and add to your stock over time.
- If you live in a cold climate and plan on stocking fish that must be moved indoors in winter, estimate the cost of their winter accommodations. You'll need an appropriately sized indoor aquarium, or you may be able to find a pet store that is willing to overwinter your fish for a fee.

In addition to budgeting for obvious elements such as pond liner, rocks, plants, and statuary, don't forget to figure in the cost of electricity to run the pump powering the falls when planning a water garden like this.

Timing

A schedule, whether your own or put together by someone you've hired, will keep the project on track. Determine a start date by deciding when you want to finish and calculate backward—but be prepared to compromise, especially when working with busy professionals.

ON YOUR OWN

In theory, you can put in a water garden anytime when you're working by yourself. However, your personal life, your climate, and the availability of materials may narrow your options. If friends are giving you a hand, you'll have to take their needs into account as well.

In cold-winter climates, you may want to plant in spring; in milder regions your aim may be to plant in autumn, before winter rains arrive. Figure out how long it will take you to get to the planting stage, allowing reasonable time to complete each step—for example, you may only want to devote a few hours each weekend to the project.

Although some features such as small ponds can be built in a weekend, don't feel obliged to work that fast. You may want to take several weeks or even longer. A large project can be spread over a year or more; however, be aware that the cost of materials may increase in that period.

USING PROFESSIONALS

If you're hiring an expert to handle the whole project, the timing may depend on that person's calendar. Landscaping projects tend to be bunched into certain months of the year, and you may have to wait to use the person you want. Because professionals often juggle more than one project at a time, there may

In cold climates, it's best not to schedule construction too tightly from late fall through early spring—in case unexpected snows throw off your plans. Downpours can similarly thwart timetables.

be "down" times when nothing's happening in your yard.

Typically, the expert will prepare a schedule for your approval. As with any outdoor work, the timing and completion of each stage will hinge on the weather. Problems with subcontractors and late delivery of materials can also throw off the schedule.

If you're hiring an expert for just part of the job, you may try to fit that person into your schedule—but more likely, the professional will fit you into his or hers. The more experts you use, the more individual schedules you must coordinate. Be prepared to be flexible and to alter your timeline as needed.

CHAPTER THREE

Equipment and Techniques

GARDEN PONDS USED TO BE CONSTRUCTED of brick or concrete, which meant hiring specialists who could do such heavy work. Today, a simple garden pond can be completed in one day by anyone who can dig a hole in the ground. Home supply stores now carry a variety of lightweight, rigid-plastic pools designed to be set directly into an excavation and filled with water. More elaborate ponds, fed by artificial waterfalls and streams, can be constructed with flexible liners and outfitted with pumps, skimmers, and underwater lights. This chapter discusses the equipment available and the wide range of water garden accessories you can install. And there are guidelines for digging, plumbing, and wiring —although you may decide to use a professional for some or all of this work. On the other hand, the low-voltage outdoor lighting described is easy for a homeowner to install.

Tools

The right tool for the right job makes the difference between enjoying a task or suffering through it. Fortunately, it doesn't take many tools—nor expensive ones—to build most of the water garden projects described in this book.

CHOOSE QUALITY TOOLS

You may already have some or all of the equipment needed, but if you do buy additional tools, choose quality over a bargain. A well-made tool handles better and lasts longer, making your job easier.

A few of the tools shown here, such as the hawk and mason's trowel, have limited and specific uses—but most of the others will serve you in many ways. Regular maintenance includes washing off dirt after use, drying the tools, and then coating the metal parts with a light oil before putting them away. Keep all of your tools free of rust and maintain sharp cutting edges.

Hawk: A lightweight aluminum hawk is used to hold mortar for numerous repair and construction projects.

Carpenter's level: Use this tool to verify both horizontal (level) and vertical (plumb) alignment.

Mason's trowel: A medium-size trowel is needed for brick and stonework.

Line level: To check level over a considerable distance, clip a line level to tightly stretched mason's twine.

Bricklayer's hammer: Use the chisel end for chipping or cutting bricks, the hammer end for tapping bricks into place.

Shovels: The long-handled shovel is the garden work-horse. D-handle shovels are best for working in tight quarters such as a small pond excavation.

Brickset: This is used for scoring and then breaking bricks.

Metal rake: A large, heavy-duty rake is useful for raking up debris and smoothing tilled soil.

Square-tipped shovel: This is essential for mixing concrete in a wheelbarrow and for scraping and leveling earth.

Hoe: Many different tasks, from weeding the garden to mixing concrete in a wheelbarrow, require a hoe.

Handsaw: The medium-size crosscut saw is best for all-around use.

Safety glasses: Keep these handy around your neck and get in the habit of putting them on for all cutting, grinding, and chipping.

Claw hammer: A claw hammer with a curved claw is primarily for finish carpentry, whereas the straight claw is preferred for construction framing.

Dust mask: Use it when cutting pressure-treated lumber, mixing cement, and in any dusty conditions.

Utility knife: Useful for cutting almost anything, this tool has replacement blades in its handle.

Rubber kneepads: Use them to protect your joints when working on your knees.

Circular saw: This is essential for any type of carpentry. A carborundum blade can be added to cut bricks, metal, and fiberglass

Drill: A cordless drill with a variety of screw-driver and drill bits will be one of your most useful tools. Pick one with 12 or more volts of power.

Adjustable wrench: Two or three wrenches of different sizes are often needed for tightening and loosening nuts and bolts.

100-foot tape: Use this when making a scale drawing of your yard and house for landscaping plans.

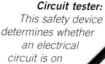

Needle-nose pliers: These are useful for any electrical work.

Circuit tester: This safety device determines whether an electrical circuit is on or off.

Outdoor extension cord: Choose cords with 12-gauge wire rather than the smaller 14-gauge. If no GFCI outlet is available (see page 51), use a cord with an in-line GFCI.

Multipurpose tool: For cutting and stripping variously sized electrical wires, this is a time saver.

Construction Safety

Building a water garden involves physical labor, tools both heavy and sharp, and electricity. All of these components require that you be extremely careful and that you coach any helpers on safety measures. An accident can happen in a number of ways—through careless tool handling, lack of eye and ear protection, improper lifting techniques, or simply not paying attention. So take a few minutes now to review some basic safety precautions.

CHECK YOUR LOCAL CODES

Before you begin any construction project in your yard, check with your building department to see what permits might be needed and what codes you will have to follow. All codes are designed to safeguard both the builders and the users of water features. They will certainly apply to electrical installations and to any piped water other than recirculating pond water.

CALL BEFORE YOU DIG

Any residential property may have buried gas, water, or electrical lines. Accidentally cutting or rupturing one of these can have catastrophic results, in terms of both damage and lawsuits. The solution is to always call before digging. Most states require that you call for clearance at least 48 hours ahead of when you dig. If you have Internet access, get the state one-call number at http://www.underspace.com/refs/ocdir.shtml. Or you can call your local gas and electric utility companies. They will provide you with a specific identification number, so that if anything does go wrong, you have a record of having checked.

CONSIDER FENCES

Because water gardens can represent a significant danger to young children (see page 28), you may need to fence off your feature. A toddler who falls into a pond or stream can drown in very little water; don't underestimate the danger.

WORK SAFELY

The following are some essential safety guidelines.

EYES Unprotected eyes are particularly vulnerable to damage during construction. Buy two or three pairs of protective glasses or goggles that fit over prescription glasses. If one pair is misplaced, you will have another ready to use. Wear them when doing anything that could send chips into your eye, such as cutting, hammering, and grinding.

EARS The noise of power tools takes a cumulative toll on your hearing. You'll protect yourself best with a high-quality pair of earmuff-style covers; at a minimum, wear rubber earplugs.

Before you begin an excavation project, it's important to determine if any water, power, or gas lines are buried on your property. Call your local utility companies for this information 48 hours in advance.

HANDS Protect your hands from blisters and scrapes, which can make it difficult to hold a tool properly. Wear work gloves when handling rough rocks, sharp wire, or wood that readily splinters.

SKIN The deep tan is no longer fashionable; it's risky. Wear sunscreen and a hat.

BACK Lift with your legs, not with your back. A bad back can incapacitate you for life. When you lift something from the ground, keep your head up and level. Looking at the horizon before you lift will force you to straighten your back. You may also consider wearing a wraparound protective back support.

WORK AREA Keep the work area clean. Pick up scrap materials so that people don't trip over them. Never leave nail points sticking out of a board. Put away tools that aren't being used.

DITCHES Never lie down to work in an excavated ditch. A surprisingly small amount of collapsing dirt can immobilize and suffocate you. During the day, fence off ditches with stakes and rope so people don't unwittingly fall in. At night, cover them with plywood. Any hole more than 5 feet deep must, by construction code, have metal or plywood shoring on both sides, held apart by spreaders.

ELECTRICAL Any outdoor receptacle must be in a weatherproof box and be controlled by a GFCI (ground fault circuit interrupter). The GFCI cuts off power in about a hundredth of a second if it detects an imbalance in the current, which usually indicates a short circuit. The GFCI can be in either the outdoor receptacle or the panel breaker. Check extension cords for damage, and don't let them lie in standing water. Always use an electrical tester to verify that a power source is off before beginning to work on it.

TOOLS Check power tool and extension cords regularly for any cuts and replace the cord as needed. Keep all cutting edges sharp: dull edges cause more accidents than sharp ones, because people use more force to cut with them. Send dull saw blades out to be sharpened. Keep all tools clean and rust free.

FIRST AID KIT Keep an adequately equipped kit handy on the job site. At a minimum it should contain eyewash liquid, large and small adhesive bandages, sterile 4-inch dressings, tape, disinfectant, and tweezers.

Excavating and Leveling

Dreaming about and planning your water garden may stir your imagination, but then reality intrudes: someone actually has to excavate the hole. Before rushing out to start digging, however, take a moment to realistically assess your health, your strength, and—perhaps most importantly—your time.

PLANNING THE EXCAVATION

Many of us have neither the inclination nor the time to dig out the soil for a garden pond or stream. However, hiring others to do the digging, and supervising them, is a viable alternative. For a larger excavation, consider calling in a professional with a small backhoe or skid-steer, commonly known as a bobcat. This will cost more, but the job will be done quickly.

REMOVING SOD

If lawn is now planted where the water feature will be located, remove the sod first. For a small area, you can cut away the sod with a square-tipped shovel or a handheld sod lifter. For larger areas, you can rent a sod cutter. This is a large, gas-powered machine that cuts 12-inch-wide strips and has an adjustable-depth cutter to get below the roots. Slice the sod into 4-foot-long sections and roll them up until you're ready to transplant or dispose of them.

WHAT WILL YOU DO WITH THE SOIL?

When you actually begin excavating, you have to put all that earth somewhere. If it's good topsoil, it may be "recycled" as another part of the overall plan (see "Don't Forget," page 39).

METHODS FOR REMOVING SOD

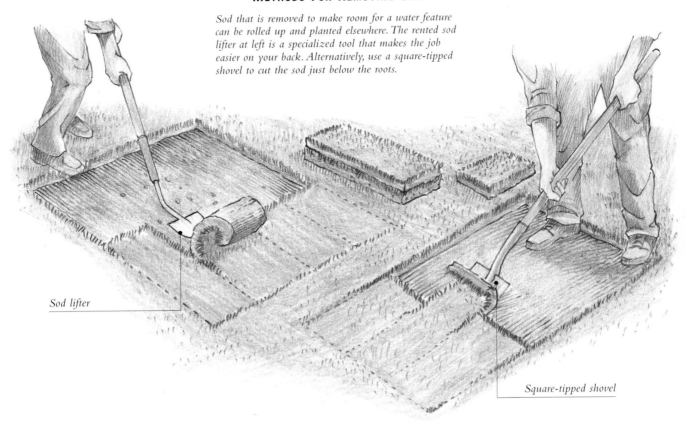

Sod that is removed to make room for a water feature can be rolled up and planted elsewhere. The rented sod lifter at left is a specialized tool that makes the job easier on your back. Alternatively, use a square-tipped shovel to cut the sod just below the roots.

Sod lifter

Square-tipped shovel

If you have a lot of rocky and poor soil to dispose of, call for a debris box: look in the yellow pages under "Debris." Most companies have boxes specifically for soil, rocks, and broken concrete. Be sure to inform the debris box company in advance that you plan to fill the box with dirt. Also let them know exactly where you want it placed, or they will just leave it on the street.

LEVELING THE GROUND

A garden pond must be level around the edges, or the pond liner will be visible on the high side. Not only is a visible liner unsightly, but exposure to the sun's ultraviolet rays will speed its disintegration. Keeping the pond perimeter level is not difficult, but it does require attention to detail as excavation progresses.

Check the level by placing a straight 2-by-4 on edge (so that it doesn't sag) with a level taped to it across the excavated area. Adjust the height of the pool perimeter as needed by digging down the high side or building up the low side. Be sure to check the level from a variety of points across the hole.

When a single 2-by-4 will not reach completely across the excavated area, you can work by checking to a stake driven into the middle of the hole. Extend your 2-by-4 and level to it, marking the point on the stake where your 2-by-4 meets it at a perfectly horizontal level; extend that mark all around the stake. Check the level against that mark at several points around the pond perimeter and either build up or lower the soil until it is level all around the excavation.

Once the perimeter is level, confirm that any plant shelves around the sides of the pond are level. They don't all have to be the same height, but they should be level to support the plant containers properly. To check that they are, just lay a level on them and use a square-tipped shovel to smooth and level the shelves' surfaces.

CHECKING FOR LEVEL

Use a straight 2-by-4 set on edge with a level on top to ensure that the pond perimeter is level all the way around. If the excavation is wider than your 2-by-4 can span, drive a stake in the center and compare the level findings from several angles. Add soil to low spots or dig down the high spots.

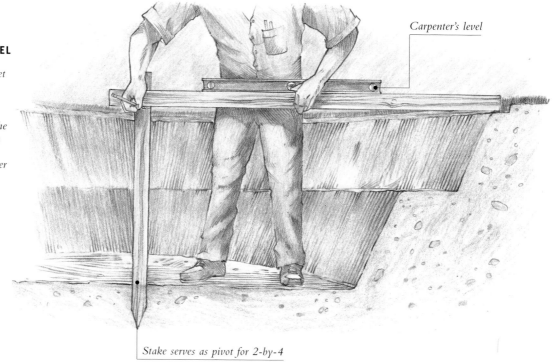

Carpenter's level

Stake serves as pivot for 2-by-4

Working on a Slope

The terrain of residential lots across the country ranges from perfectly flat to extremely steep. If your best site for a pond is on sloping ground, you can address the problem by either terracing a small area or adding one or more retaining walls.

TERRACES

If a hillside rises outside of your back door, you have the natural makings for a combination waterfall, stream, and pond. If all of your ground is irregular or hilly, you may choose to install a series of small pools with water cascading from one to the other. All you need to master in this case are some basic terracing techniques.

On gently sloping ground, you can create a natural-looking shallow pond by leveling a section large enough for the pond and forming a berm, or raised earthen bank, with the excavated dirt on the downhill side. (See "Creating a Berm" on page 41.) This technique requires only a moderate amount of digging, but you must be sure to stabilize the fill dirt in the berm. Pack the earth firmly and plant it with deeply rooted plants to prevent movement in the event of heavy rains.

Whenever a pond is installed on or at the bottom of a slope, rainwater coming down the hill should be directed away from it. The runoff is commonly controlled by a berm along the high side or by a perforated drainpipe laid in a gravel-filled ditch just above the pond (see "Drainage" illustration on page 85). The pipe should drop about 1 inch for every 10 feet in order to carry the water off to a natural drain or storm sewer.

The longer the slope and the wetter your climate, the more carefully you will need to control water runoff.

RETAINING WALLS

A retaining wall is specifically that: a wall designed to retain the earth and prevent it from sliding down a slope. Retaining walls may be built both below and above the area terraced for a pond or waterfall—or one can suffice above the pond, with a berm on the downslope side. Retaining walls must be built to withstand the pressure behind them generated by water and water-saturated soil.

Any retaining wall over 4 feet high should be designed by a licensed structural engineer to ensure its safety. Additionally, check with your building department to see if a building permit is needed and what construction codes must be met.

Retaining walls can be constructed from materials such as pressure-treated boards or timbers, dry stacked rocks, mortared brick or stone, or a variety of modular masonry units available in home supply centers. Depending on the manufacturer, you can often create a modular wall footing by simply reversing the bottom row of blocks – turning them upside down with the exterior side facing inward. Here are some guidelines to help you if you are doing the work yourself.

TERRACED RETAINING WALLS

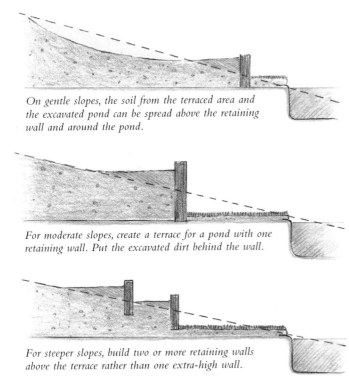

On gentle slopes, the soil from the terraced area and the excavated pond can be spread above the retaining wall and around the pond.

For moderate slopes, create a terrace for a pond with one retaining wall. Put the excavated dirt behind the wall.

For steeper slopes, build two or more retaining walls above the terrace rather than one extra-high wall.

A Modular Retaining Wall

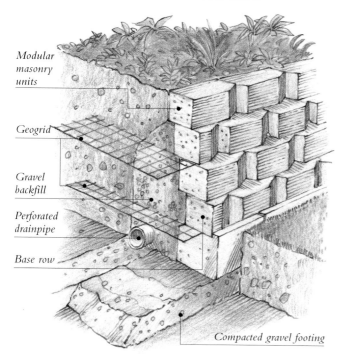

Modular masonry units

Geogrid

Gravel backfill

Perforated drainpipe

Base row

Compacted gravel footing

Proper retaining wall construction includes the following:

- Foundation: Put the wall on a solid foundation, which can range from 4 inches of compacted gravel in a ditch to a layer of stones embedded below grade to a poured concrete footing. If you live in a cold climate, be sure the footing ditch is dug below the frost line, or ground heave in the winter may topple the wall. Check local codes to see how deep it needs to be and if reinforcing bars are required in the footing.
- Battered wall: As the wall goes up, it must be sloped back, or battered, to withstand the forces behind it. Many modular units lock together with built-in batter.
- Starting point: On irregular ground, start building the wall at the lowest spot. Where the wall must step up, increase the height by only one course at a time.
- Drainage: Drains must be installed behind the wall to keep water from collecting there. Dig a drainage ditch behind the footing, lay down 3 inches of gravel, install a rigid or flexible perfo-

rated drainpipe with the holes facing down, and backfill with gravel as the wall goes up. As extra insurance, you can install weep holes through the wall at least every 3 feet to permit water to drain through the front. If runoff still threatens to enter the pond, add a second drainpipe between the wall and the pond.

Walls with extra pressure behind them due to a steep slope or constantly wet soil may need additional anchoring. Here are three ways to supply extra support:

- Geogrid: This strong, flexible material is embedded between wall courses and extends several feet back into the excavated bank, where it is buried to anchor the wall (see left).
- Vertical posts: A wall of horizontally placed pressure-treated timbers often needs vertical posts in front, sunk deeply and spaced evenly across the wall, to keep it from tipping forward (see below).
- Deadmen: These horizontal T-shaped anchors are buried in the slope behind a timber wall and pinned to one or more courses with reinforcing bars driven through holes drilled in the ends of the deadmen.

Vertical Post and Deadmen

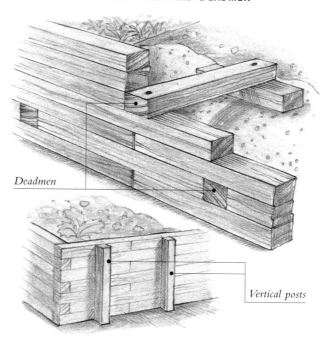

Deadmen

Vertical posts

Pipes, Fittings, and Valves

The plumbing needed for ponds with pumps is fairly straightforward: it comes down to an assortment of fittings, pipes, and valves. These are used to connect and control water lines that run from the pump to a fountain, waterfall, or stream head. Piping is also employed to resupply pond water lost to evaporation. Keep in mind that water flows best when it can flow straight. Use pipe with a smooth interior and minimize sharp turns for the most efficient water flow in your layout.

PIPES

The most widely used piping and tubing materials for ponds and waterfalls are rigid PVC, clear vinyl or black vinyl tubing, and corrugated black vinyl pipe. For long, straight supply runs, rigid PVC pipe is best, but within the pond itself, flexible tubing is easier to work with, particularly when it must be bent over, around, and under other objects. Here are some details to help you choose the best types for your project.

RIGID PVC Easy to cut and assemble, this is the pipe used to carry water underground from a source to a garden pond. Buy either Schedule 40 or Class 200 pipe; both are stronger than other varieties and less likely to break and leak after installation. They are sold in 20-foot lengths and can be easily cut with a hacksaw or special PVC shears.

CLEAR VINYL This tubing is best used for short runs because its relatively thin walls kink and compress easily. It blends well with its surroundings due to its transparency. Exposure to sunlight can cause algae to build up inside the walls.

BLACK VINYL The black color helps control the buildup of any algae in the pipe, and it is nearly invisible underwater. However, if bent too sharply or compressed under rocks, it will restrict water flow.

CORRUGATED BLACK VINYL This is a kink-free hose that can bend at sharp angles and does not compress. The interior is smooth, so water flow is not restricted. Similar to this is flexible PVC piping, which also readily bends around and under obstacles.

FITTINGS

Pipes are joined together and to pumps or other devices with fittings. Rigid-pipe fittings are generally slipped over the pipe and glued in place. Some rigid-pipe fittings are threaded on one end for connecting to the pump, with slip-joints on the other end. Flexible-pipe fittings go inside the pipe and are held in place by raised ridges. These are known as barb fittings. Stainless steel hose clamps are sometimes added to ensure that the hose and fitting do not separate.

Rigid PVC

Clear vinyl

Black vinyl

Corrugated black vinyl

Hose clamps

Fittings are not all standard sizes, so double-check your pipe and fitting sizes before you make your purchases.

T FITTING Used to direct water in two opposite directions or to allow water to flow straight ahead and also make a 90-degree turn, such as when installing a branch line.

ELBOW Comes in 90-degree and 45-degree versions, with either sharp or sweeping bends; two 45-degree elbows rather than one 90-degree elbow cause less friction, and hence improve the flow around corners.

T fitting

Elbow

COUPLING Used to join pipe or tubing.

Coupling

VALVES

Valves control the flow of water—limiting it in some cases, maximizing it in others, or shutting off the water completely. A valve between the water source and the pond is useful when the pond must be drained and cleaned. Some common valves are shown here.

FLOAT VALVE A float valve, similar to those in toilet tanks, is connected to a water supply to maintain a constant water level. Because the water it releases into the pond as the water level drops is untreated, you have to add a detoxifier for chlorine or chloramine.

Although float valves are often enclosed in the skimmer (see page 108) with the pump, some specialists prefer placement at the opposite end of the pond, so that the chlorine/chloramine

Float valve

Three-way valve

Gate valve

Ball valve

detoxifiers can do their job before water enters the biofilter (see page 58). Float valves should be shut off for at least one week a year, so that you can determine the approximate amount of water loss and refilling needed and thus calculate the proper amount of detoxifier to be added.

THREE-WAY VALVE Like a T fitting, it controls the water flow in two directions at once. It's better than using two ball valves (see below), as it is impossible to inadvertently shut off the water. Use this when the pool filter and waterfall are on the same pump.

GATE VALVE These valves shut off the water entirely and will not leak. They are usually completely open or completely closed, although they can also be used to control water flow.

BALL VALVE These are quick-opening and -closing valves, often requiring just a half-turn of the handle. They are excellent for controlling water flow, but on less expensive models they may not completely shut off the water.

Filters

The purpose of a pond filter is to keep the water clean. Most water garden problems begin with ammonia, which forms from fish waste, decaying organic matter, and uneaten fish food. Even low doses of ammonia can be toxic to fish. As a result, most ponds with fish and few plants need to be filtered to keep the water clear and healthy. Nature has its own filtration methods (see "The Nitrogen Cycle" on page 164), but most backyard fish ponds are home to many more fish than would survive in a similar volume of water in nature, and therefore need some help.

TYPES OF FILTERS

Two types of pond filters are used in water gardens: mechanical and biological. Mechanical filters trap solid matter in the water. Biological filters, or biofilters, can do the same but also have microorganisms that remove toxic waste from the water.

MECHANICAL FILTERS strain pond water through one of several different media, such as foam pads or screens. These filters are often attached to the pump and they should be removed and cleaned on a regular schedule. Mechanical filters remove solids from the water, but they do not remove wastes that are toxic to fish.

BIOLOGICAL FILTERS house large numbers of beneficial bacteria that remove toxins as the water passes steadily over them. The bacteria live on media inside the filter, which are specially designed to support a maximum amount of bacteria. To keep the bacteria alive, water should be pumped through the filter 24 hours a day. Biofilters have a "safe-flow" rate and the pump should not be too powerful or the filter will be ineffective.

Biological filters must be cleaned periodically—typically once every month or two. How filters are cleaned depends on their design; some have a back-flush system, and others must be sprayed and agitated to remove solids that build up on the beads. No biofilter should be cleaned with water containing chlorine or chloramine, as these chemicals will kill the beneficial bacteria (see "Harmful Chemicals" on page 165). Use sludge-digesting bacteria to decrease the burden of cleaning a biofilter.

BIOLOGICAL FILTER

Pond water enters from the lower right and passes over plastic disks holding bacteria colonies for biological filtration. Gravel holds everything in place and adds another level of filtration. The water is then returned to the pond through the pipe at upper left.

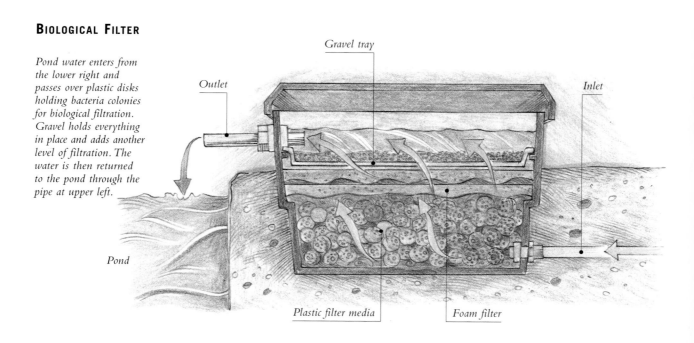

Gravel tray

Outlet

Inlet

Pond

Plastic filter media

Foam filter

A balance of mechanical and biological filters, coupled with oxygen-producing plants, maintains the clear water of this pond, to the enjoyment of fish and owners alike. Chemical treatments will also keep pond water clear, but some are poisonous to fish.

FILTRATION RATE

The rule of thumb is to pump a minimum of half the volume of a fish pond through a filter every hour for large ponds, and the entire volume for ponds under 1,000 gallons. Koi ponds, which usually have much larger fish, should be filtered entirely every hour regardless of size. Ponds that receive full sun should also be filtered more often.

SKIMMERS

A skimmer is a device designed to remove floating debris, large and small, before it sinks to the bottom. It is simply a submerged box attached to the suction (inlet) side of a pump that draws a thin film of water over an opening and traps pollen, dust, and larger debris in a net (see page 108).

ULTRAVIOLET WATER CLARIFIERS

One way to make green pond water clear is to supplement the filtration system with an ultraviolet water clarifier. These devices kill single-celled floating algae, but

Ultraviolet clarifier

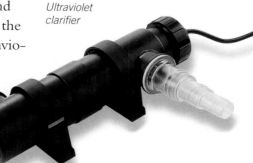

not the beneficial side- and bottom-growing algae. They also cause floating particles to clump together so they can be picked up by the filters more readily. Both submersible and external models of UV clarifiers are available.

WATER TREATMENTS

To kill pathogenic bacteria in drinking water, many municipal water districts are switching from chlorine to chloramine, a mixture of chlorine and ammonia that is considered a better disinfectant. Although not harmful to humans and other mammals, both chlorine and chloramine pose a serious threat to fish, shellfish, and reptiles by reducing their ability to process oxygen. (See "Harmful Chemicals" on page 165.)

For pools or streams that have no fish or plant life, chlorine will keep the water sparkling clear by killing all algae—the main culprit behind green water. Other fish- and plant-safe chemicals, such as flocculants and certain algicides, can supplement and even enhance biological filters. Bacterial additives are also available to condition biological filters and to consume organic debris, thus helping keep filters clean. Finally, ocean salt, added to ponds at a rate of 8 pounds per 1,000 gallons, is a partial algae control in addition to being beneficial to fish health.

Pumps

Garden pond pumps serve several purposes: they circulate the water, thereby aerating it; they clean the water by pumping it through filters; and they lift water from the pond to a waterfall or a fountain, which also helps aerate the water. One pump will generally suffice for all these tasks.

PUMPS FOR ALL PURPOSES

If you plan on a pond with a biological filter installed at a waterfall, the pump should run constantly. The filter should have the entire pond volume pumped through it about once an hour; half that rate is needed if you don't have a waterfall.

If you want to turn off the waterfall at night, add a T fitting to the pipe coming out of your filter. Direct one line from the T

to the waterfall and let the other line run into the pond with an air bubbler (called a venturi) attached, for added aeration. Install valves just beyond the T to both lines so you can control the water flow as needed.

There are three basic types of water pumps: submersible, in-line (also called external or surface), and the combination in-line/submersible pump.

SUBMERSIBLE PUMPS are available in two forms: they are either powered by 120-volt household current or the safer, easy-to-install, 12-volt current. They must be completely underwater when operating or the motor will quickly burn out. Any submerged pump should

It takes a properly sized pump to provide enough pressure and lift to keep a pond, stream, and waterfall functioning well. Most pumps specify how many gallons per hour they pump and the head, or height, to which they can lift water.

be placed on a couple of bricks or otherwise protected from drawing in fine grit and other debris from the bottom of the pond that can clog and damage the impeller assembly.

Submersible pump

IN-LINE PUMPS are for surface use only and must be placed near the pond in a location that does not flood. Although they can be exposed to the weather without harm, they must never be submerged. This type is available in larger sizes than submersible pumps are.

Combination in-line/submersible pump

COMBINATION IN-LINE/ SUBMERSIBLE PUMPS operate equally well underwater or on land. They are widely used in water gardens because they are quiet, easy to install, energy efficient, and available in many styles. Depending on the model, they are capable of pumping from about 80 to more than 3,000 gallons per hour.

In-line pump

Powering a Waterfall

How powerful a pump you'll need depends on whether or not you'll have a waterfall. If you need only to recirculate pond water through filters, the pump's GPH must be sufficient to circulate—at a minimum—one-half of the pond's volume per hour (see "Filtration Rate," page 59, for the relevant variables). If the pump will power a waterfall, however, you also need to know the height, or head, of the falls and how much water you want flowing over them. Here's how to figure the pump size for your waterfall feature.

Step 1. Determine how many gallons of water are in your pond (see "Water Volume," page 36).

Step 2. Measure how many feet above the pump the spillway will be. To account for friction loss, add another foot for each 10 feet of tubing from pump to waterfall.

Step 3. Decide how much water at a time you want flowing over the spillway. Conveniently enough, the average pond's volume recirculated once an hour

happens to look just right spilling over the average waterfall. But if you want more flow, hold a garden hose over the falls and turn the faucet until you like the effect; collect that flow in a container of known capacity and calculate the GPH from the time required to fill it. For example, if it takes 45 seconds to fill a 5-gallon bucket, you'll need a pump that recirculates 400 GPH for the head of your falls (60 seconds × 60 minutes divided by 45 seconds × 5 gallons = 400 GPH).

Step 4. Purchase a pump with a GPH that will circulate at least half of the pond's volume each hour while raising an acceptable amount of water to your waterfall height. Pumps are generally sized according to their GPH rate at a height of 1 foot. The higher the head, the lower the GPH pumped. Usually, the GPH at different heads is printed on the product's label (see page 62). In general, you should select a pump that will exceed your needs. If necessary, you can restrict the flow rate over a waterfall by partially closing a valve, but you cannot increase a pump's existing flow rate.

SELECTING A PUMP

Because there are all sorts of different pumps on the market, selecting the best one for your purpose can be confusing. Here are some features to look for.

PERFORMANCE CHART This information on the label tells you how many gallons per hour (GPH) of water the pump will move at a certain "head" height, or elevation above the surface. The better pumps list the volume flow at different heads, rather than just a maximum flow and head (see the chart below).

POWER USAGE Because biofilters require that the pump run continually, energy cost can become a decisive factor in your choice.

If your provider charged 11 cents per kilowatt hour (check your bill for your actual rate), an energy-efficient pump model with a capacity of 1,200 gallons per hour at a 1-foot head would cost you about $11 per month in electricity.

MAGNETIC DRIVE OPTION Increasingly popular electromagnetic drive pumps are available for submersible, combination, and in-line pumps. Magnetic drive pumps require neither oil nor bearings—and therefore no seal—which means far less maintenance and no worries about oil leaks. These pumps are virtually friction free and the most energy efficient of all types.

CORD LENGTH Check the length of the power cord to be sure it will reach your power source without requiring an extension cord or a spliced length of wire.

OUTLET AND TUBING Water is drawn into the pump through the inlet and then discharged via the outlet. The outlet is connected to the tubing or pipe carrying the water to the head of your stream, fountain, or waterfall. If you haven't purchased an all-inclusive kit, make sure the pipes or tubing you buy match the size of the outlet on your pump.

This kit includes a submersible pump and filter, a cord, and a fountain jet.

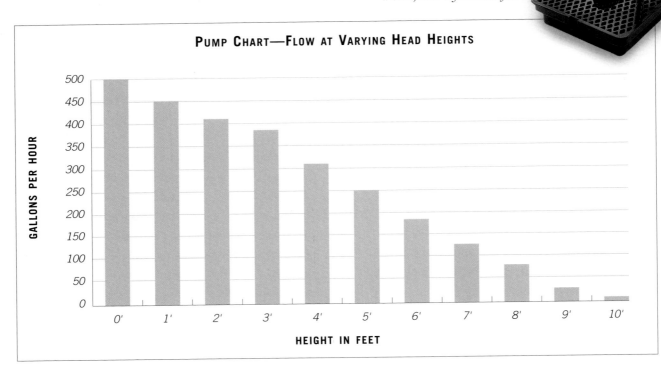

PUMP CHART—FLOW AT VARYING HEAD HEIGHTS

GALLONS PER HOUR (y-axis: 0, 50, 100, 150, 200, 250, 300, 350, 400, 450, 500)

HEIGHT IN FEET (x-axis: 0', 1', 2', 3', 4', 5', 6', 7', 8', 9', 10')

Outdoor Lighting

Outdoor lighting allows you to significantly expand your living area by illuminating a deck, patio, or garden area for nighttime use. And a lighted yard means a water garden can be seen and enjoyed from inside the house as well.

PLANNING OUTDOOR LIGHTING

When planning your outdoor lighting, consider that you will be creating an atmosphere, not simply lighting the yard. Two 100-watt floodlights mounted above a door may illuminate the yard, but that is not outdoor lighting. Subtlety is the key to success here.

Before purchasing any equipment, take some flashlights into the yard at night to get a rough idea of what you want to light. Place one in a position to light a plant or tree near the water garden and then back away to view it from a distance. Various sizes of flashlights with adjustable beams help you get a sense of what you want to accomplish.

DRAWING THE PLAN

The next step is to create a scale drawing of your yard on ¼-inch graph paper (where ¼ inch equals 1 foot). Use a 100-foot tape to measure your lot perimeter and then draw in the house, shrubs, trees, fences, and the water feature. Also note the nearest 120-volt receptacles, which you will need to plug in a low-voltage transformer. With this information in hand, you will be able to determine how long the electrical wiring runs will be and just how many lamps you will need.

WATER LIGHTING

Ponds can be lit dramatically both on the surface and underwater. (For underwater lights to have maximum effect, however, the pond water needs to be clear.) Sealed underwater lights have long cords and weighted bases. The better ones are

Underwater lights make a garden stream magical, particularly as dusk turns to dark. These lights come in a variety of wattages and bulbs. Underwater lights can be either 120 volts or part of a low-voltage system; many have adjustable beams and color filters.

adjustable, so that you can angle the light for the best effect. Pond lights are commonly made of plastic, fiberglass, or bronze.

In streams, lights placed at ground level will cast the ripples in strong relief, emphasizing the water's movement.

For a waterfall, position a light behind the water if possible, or up into the falling water from below.

Outdoor lighting on this rocky stream adds nighttime drama to the water feature. For best effect, lighted water gardens should be viewable from within the house as well as from a porch or patio.

Lighting Systems

There are four ways to set up outdoor lighting: 120-volt (an extension of the household wiring), low-voltage, solar, and light-emitting diodes, or LEDs. Of the four, the safe 12-volt, or low-voltage, system is the least expensive and most practical.

WHICH SYSTEM IS FOR YOU?

Running 120-volt wiring outdoors can be quite complex and generally requires hiring a licensed electrician. LEDs and solar lighting continue to grow in popularity but may not offer the diversity and capabilities of low-voltage lights.

120-VOLT WIRING These days, 120-volt house wiring is rarely used for outdoor lighting itself, but instead provides the current for a low-voltage system. This generally means installing one or more 120-volt outdoor

receptacles in your yard for a low-voltage transformer and for any other 120-volt equipment, such as pumps.

LOW-VOLTAGE LIGHTING Outdoor lighting has been revolutionized by low-voltage systems. Home-owners with little wiring or lighting knowledge can install these set-ups safely (see page 67). Although they are only 12 volts in power, the illumination is as bright as standard 120-volt lights.

SOLAR LIGHTING Solar technology continues to advance in both design and quality, but it still does not offer the diversity of low-voltage lighting. Solar lights have photovoltaic cells on the lamp that recharge a small battery in the lamp during daylight hours. Although these lights must be in full-sun locations to charge adequately, they are excellent choices for lighting areas that cannot be reached by

ABOVE: *Solar lights have no bothersome cords, so they can be relocated easily whenever the need arises.*
LEFT: *Sealed underwater lights cast an entirely new perspective on waterfalls. This low-voltage light can be placed in front of the falling water, directly under it, or behind it.*

low-voltage lights. Another advantage of solar lights is their portability: you just pick up the fixture and move it wherever you'd like it, with no wiring concerns. Solar lights, however, produce significantly less light than low-voltage systems and are more atmospheric than functional.

LED Light-emitting diodes are relatively new to the outdoor lighting industry but are gaining in popularity. They are solid-state devices that require a small pulse of electricity from a battery to light up the diode. LEDs will long outlast a standard incandescent bulb, but each one produces only about a tenth of a watt of power. These are handy for small accent lights, but not for complete landscape lighting. A great

advantage of LEDs, however, is that because they lack delicate bulb filaments, they can take rough treatment without failing.

Electrical Permits and Safety

Extending house wiring to the yard normally requires a permit. Your building department may also require that a licensed electrical contractor install the wiring—or at least sign off on it. After you obtain a permit, be sure to have an inspector confirm that the installation meets all appropriate electrical codes.

Safety is an important consideration in any electrical wiring project, but particularly so in outdoor applications. The National Electric Code requires that all outdoor switches and receptacles have weatherproof covers and that the receptacles be protected with a GFCI (see "Electrical" on page 51). Also, electrical outlets cannot be within 10 feet of a water feature. Of course, the cardinal safety rule to observe is never to work on a live circuit.

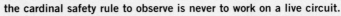

Outdoor lighting not only adds beauty but provides security. The stream near the walkway is clearly visible to visitors arriving after dark.

Low-Voltage Lighting Equipment

Only low-voltage lighting is discussed in detail here, because it is the most versatile and most practical of all outdoor lighting systems. The equipment is rapidly evolving and expanding, so spend a few hours at an outdoor lighting store to familiarize yourself with all the styles available before deciding what will best serve your needs.

KITS VERSUS COMPONENTS

Low-voltage lighting can be purchased in a kit form or as individual components. For a simple setup—and one that can be installed in an hour or so—kits are a good choice. For $50 to $100 you get a transformer, about 100 feet of wire, and 6 to 12 lights of varying styles, usually basic tiered lights with a couple of spotlights.

Kit transformers, however, are usually designed to supply only the lamps included in the kit; adding more will overload the transformer. By selecting the wiring, transformer, and lamps individually, you get a much wider selection.

EQUIPMENT NEEDS

A low-voltage lighting system has just four basic elements: a transformer, wiring, lamps, and bulbs. Installing the system is both safe and uncomplicated.

TRANSFORMERS Low-voltage systems depend on a transformer, which reduces standard 120-volt household current to a harmless 12 volts. The transformer is then plugged into a 120-volt outlet, and low-voltage wiring is run from it to each lamp.

Transformer models vary in capacity, handling anywhere from 50 to 1,000 watts or more. Some transformers have two or more circuits, which can supply power to separate lighting areas. Before purchasing a transformer, add up the number of watts for all the bulbs you plan to use. It's wise to get a transformer that will handle at least 50 percent more than that, because once you see the effect in your landscape, you'll probably want to expand the system.

The higher-end transformers include timers to control the hours of use and a photoelectric cell that turns the lights on at dusk and off at dawn. Some also have a memory chip that restores the lighting schedule in the event of a power outage.

WIRING Low-voltage lighting kits commonly come with 14-gauge wires, which are sufficient only for the limited area they will cover. If you're designing your own system, select a thicker wire. (The lower the gauge number, the thicker the wire.) Thicker wire will ensure better-performing lights at the end of the run. Generally, 14-gauge wire is sufficient for lamps adding up to 200 watts; for more than that, use 12-gauge wire.

LAMPS Low-end lamps are made of plastic; high-end lamps may be of copper, bronze, or brass. There are countless styles of lamps, but most fall into the following categories.

- Tiered: Also called pagoda or path lamps, they are commonly used to downlight paths and driveways.
- Spotlights: These are ideal for placing high in a tree to create a moonlight effect, or for angling up from the ground to light a tree from below.
- Floodlights: When a broad area, such as an entire stream and waterfall, is to be lit, these are a good choice.
- Underwater lights: These watertight lamps are designed to be placed directly into a garden pond or behind a waterfall.
- Riser lights: Ideal for deck steps, they are set into the stair riser to provide extra safety when negotiating stairs.

BULBS The best bulbs for low-voltage systems are halogen bulbs; the inert gas allows them to burn brighter and more efficiently. They also last much longer than do standard incandescent bulbs. Their wattage ranges from 10 to 100, but the most widely used bulbs are in the 20- to 50-watt range.

Halogen bulbs, however, must not be touched during installation. The trace oils on your fingertips will cause the bulb to burst as it heats up. Cover your fingers with a tissue when you insert them. If you do touch a bulb, clean it with a cloth dipped in rubbing alcohol before turning on the lamp.

LOW-VOLTAGE INSTALLATION

Lay out the light fixtures and wire according to your plan—beside pathways, under and in trees, and in the water features.

Use one wire for lights that will be in water and a separate wire for lights on land.

Wires can be laid directly on the ground or buried. Where wire must cross the lawn, use a square-tipped shovel to cut and pry open the sod about 6 inches deep, push the wire down with a stick, and then press the slot closed with your foot.

Most low-voltage wiring is connected to the lamps with press-on connectors. But for more reliable connections, strip the ends of the wires and join them with waterproof wire nuts that twist over the wire ends. These nuts are usually available wherever you bought the light-

ing equipment. You can also join wires by twisting them together and then covering them with a special rubber tube that shrinks when heated, to seal the connection (see Step 3 on page 79).

Mount the transformer near a 120-volt outlet at the house or in the garden, and connect the low-voltage wiring to the transformer. If there is a photocell, adjust it to face southwest, making sure it catches the most light possible. This will ensure that the lights don't come on before dusk and waste electricity.

Once the system is installed, turn it on, verify that all lights are working, and adjust the lamp angles as needed.

INSTALLING LOW-VOLTAGE EQUIPMENT

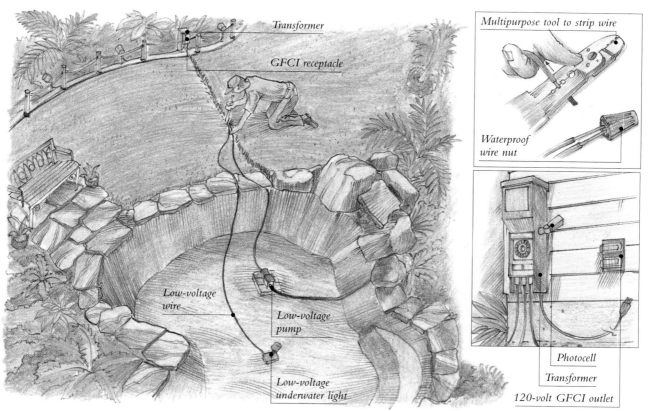

Transformer

GFCI receptacle

Multipurpose tool to strip wire

Waterproof wire nut

Low-voltage wire

Low-voltage pump

Low-voltage underwater light

Photocell

Transformer

120-volt GFCI outlet

Pond Edgings

Quality edging not only gives form to the pond, it also helps define the style. Precisely aligned brick edging, for instance, is highly formal; irregular rock edging is more informal and naturalistic.

EDGING CHOICES

Edging serves several practical functions. It protects the pond from damage, hides the material used to form the pond, and helps keep debris from washing into the water. No matter what edging you select, the effect can be softened with the addition of plants along the perimeter and in the water.

ROCKS Large and small rocks—often with plants interspersed among them—are the most widely used pond edging. This edging looks even more natural if several of the largest rocks are partly submerged. In a pond with a flexible liner, you'd do this by digging a slightly backward-sloping shelf around the pool perimeter, 3 to 8 inches deep and 8 to 16 inches wide, depending on the size of the rocks you select. Place the liner over this, set the rocks in place, and trim off any excess liner.

Rigid-liner ponds typically have rocks projecting an inch or two over their edges to hide the liner and protect it from ultraviolet light. If the ground is particularly soft around the pond, you may have to compact 3 or 4 inches of crushed rock around the edge to support the rocks and keep them from deforming the liner (see "Rock Edging" on facing page.)

CONCRETE For long-lasting edging around either a rigid-liner or flexible-liner pool, use concrete. One method is to dig a 6-inch-wide trench about 6 inches deep around the proposed pond perimeter before the pool is excavated; this is then filled with concrete that will support large rocks placed beside the pond, or it can be covered by bricks or paving (see "Poured-Concrete Wall" on facing page). The concrete's stability also allows people to walk beside the pool without damaging the bank.

GRASS Perhaps the most natural-looking pond edging is grass. However, depending on the proportions involved, lawn that runs right up to the water's edge can look odd. Another drawback is that mowing must be done very carefully, or too much debris will drift into the pond. One solution is to separate the lawn from the pond with wild grasses or native water plants (see

Edging sets the tone of a water garden. Here, the straight lines and careful masonry work lend formality to the pond and the surrounding walkways. Ponds lined with boulders, on the other hand, appear more rustic and casual.

pages 144–153 for ideas). If you're set on lawn meeting pond, you'll need to support the edge so that the bank doesn't eventually collapse from people walking on it. Dig a narrow trench, about 3 inches wide and 6 inches deep, around the edge of the pond and fill it with concrete; then let the grass grow over it to hide it (see below).

STONE WALLS For a more formal pool edging, and one with great durability, choose brick, flagstone, or pavers. Any material that is mortared must be placed on a concrete footing to prevent the material from moving and cracking the grout.

Dig a shelf about 12 inches deep around the pool's edge and pour a 3-inch-thick concrete footing. Then build a stone wall on top of the footing, as shown below. Because the footing is poured into a ditch dug into the shelf, no forms are needed to contain the concrete. The flexible liner can go either behind the stone wall and footing or in front of it, under the cap.

ROCK EDGING

POURED-CONCRETE WALL

Pour a concrete edge before pond excavation.

GRASS EDGING

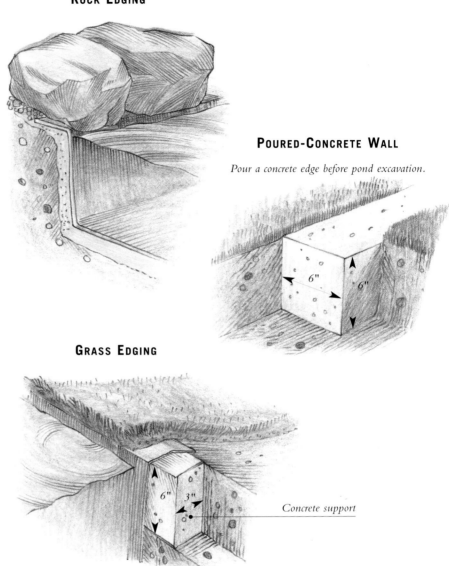

Concrete support

STONE WALL

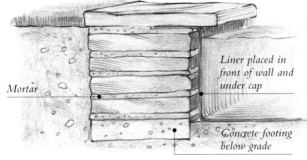

Mortar

Liner placed in front of wall and under cap

Concrete footing below grade

Build a wall of stone or concrete pavers after excavating.

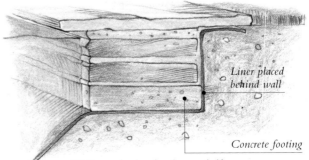

Liner placed behind wall

Concrete footing

Wall can also be placed on a shelf.

Crossings

Streams and ponds seem made to be crossed. After all, who can resist finding out what's on the other side? A crossing may be a gently curved bridge, large rocks conveniently placed in the water, or simply two logs with a decking formed by stout limbs. There are many ways to cross water, as described below.

STEPPING-STONES

For a stream or shallow pond, stepping-stones probably make the most natural crossing. For deeper ponds, you will need to place them on piers built up beneath the water. In most cases, stepping-stones are planned and built before any water is added to the pond.

Stepping-stones must be firmly positioned, so that they will not move when weight is placed on them. A round-bottomed stone can be stabilized on top of a flexible liner by securing it in a bed of mortar.

Stepping-stones made of exposed-aggregate concrete may be primarily for the sure of foot, but they also help direct the eyes to take in different vistas across the pond.

(The mortar can be disguised by embedding smaller rocks in it.)

If the rock is large and stable enough to stand by itself, pad it underneath with something like old carpet to protect the liner.

For stepping-stones that cross a deeper area, build piers with mortared bricks as shown below. The pier itself rests on a concrete footing poured beneath the flexible liner. Set the first row of bricks on a 1-inch-thick mortar base on the liner. Use four bricks for each course and stag-

ger the layout so that mortar joints are not aligned one above the other.

The top course of the pier should be just flush with the water surface: adjust the height of the bricks with more or less mortar, or insert half-thickness bricks as needed. Top the pier with a stepping stone only slightly larger than the pier. Set the stone on a 1-inch-thick mortar bed and tap it firmly with a rubber mallet to set it; then check that it is level. Let the mortar cure for three days before filling the pond.

BRIDGES

A bridge is more than just a means to cross water. It is a place to stop and daydream while viewing your water feature from a new perspective. Bridges can be made of wood, concrete, steel, or stone, but wood is most commonly used because of its lower cost, versatility, and availability.

STEPPING-STONE PIERS

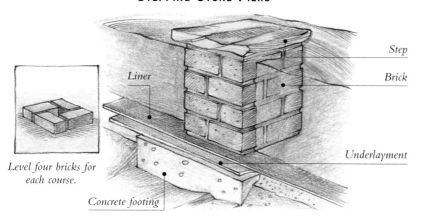

Level four bricks for each course.

Liner

Step

Brick

Underlayment

Concrete footing

BRIDGE SPANS The first rule in building a bridge is to determine what distance the supporting wood beams can safely span while carrying the weight of one or more people. There are complex span charts for different wood species and lumber sizes, but use these guidelines for a safe 3-foot-wide bridge: A 4-foot span requires 2-by-4s for the bridge span; a 6-foot span needs 2-by-6s; an 8-foot span needs 2-by-8s; and so on. If additional strength, is needed, you can double the size of the bridge spans by nailing two 2-by pieces together or you can add a third span down the center of the bridge.

BRIDGE FOOTINGS For durability, a bridge must be securely anchored on both ends, so that it neither moves nor rests in water or on damp ground. The tricky part is getting the footings level. A simple solution is to build 2-by-4 forms slightly wider than the bridge, level them, and then fill them with ready-mix concrete. To keep the bridge from moving, set two short lengths of reinforcing bar into the concrete before it hardens. Position the rebar so it will fall under the ends of the bridge spans, drill holes in the spans, and set them over the rebar (see above).

RAILINGS Even though a short and low bridge may not need railings, they lend a sense of security to those crossing it.

BASIC WOOD BRIDGE

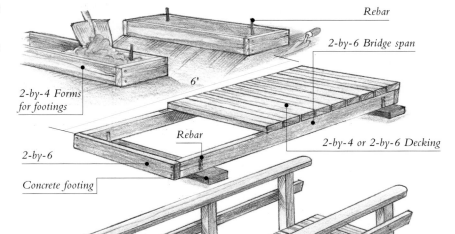

Rebar

2-by-6 Bridge span

2-by-4 Forms for footings

6'

Rebar

2-by-4 or 2-by-6 Decking

2-by-6

Concrete footing

Use 4-by-4 material for the posts and through-bolt these into the spans. Notch the decking boards so the posts are flush with the spans. Make the top railing from 2-by-6 material and add one or two horizontal rails as desired (see above).

DECKING The bridge decking should be of a rot-resistant wood such as cedar or redwood lumber. Space the deck boards apart by the thickness of a 16-penny nail to allow for shrinking and swelling through the seasons. Extend the ends of the decking over the spans on each side by 2 inches. Fasten the decking with hot-dipped galvanized nails or vinyl-coated decking screws.

If the bridge will be more than 3 feet wide, add a center span between the two outer ones.

TOXIC PRODUCTS

You should be aware that certain construction materials or finishes can potentially stress or kill pond fish. For example, concrete will cause the pH level to rise; pressure-treated wood may contain high levels of arsenic; and sealants may be toxic until they chemically cure. Such materials should not be in contact with pond water, nor positioned so that rain runs off of them into the pond. Always check with the supplier or manufacturer of the products you use to ensure that they are fish safe.

CHAPTER FOUR

Water Garden Projects

ONCE THE PLANNING AND DESIGN STAGES of your water garden project are behind you and you've absorbed the techniques described in the last chapter, you can start putting what you've learned to work. In this chapter we'll take you step by step through a number of projects, from attractive small fountains to more elaborate ponds, streams, and waterfalls. For each one, we've provided detailed instructions and photographs or illustrations to guide you through the project. Some cases call for a considerable amount of work—digging out ponds, for instance, or moving rocks for streams and waterfalls. If you prefer not to do the labor, you can apply all the knowledge you've acquired to work out a detailed plan for others to follow. Either way, you'll end up with the water feature you desire.

Bamboo Water Garden

Almost any watertight pot or bowl can become a miniature water garden to enjoy in your home, on the patio, or by the front door. You can find the small pump, plastic tubing, and bamboo fountain at water garden suppliers. If you opt to make your own bamboo spout, you must drill through the bamboo's joints with a long bit.

1 **Attach one end** of the tubing to the submersible pump. The pump box usually indicates the diameter of tubing needed, so check that before purchasing the tubing. Depending on the size of your bowl, add one or two bricks to support plants.

2 **Run the tubing** through the main piece of bamboo and pull a few inches out of the hole where the spout will fit. Direct the tubing into the spout and secure the spout into the main piece of bamboo. Position the fountain assembly on the bowl.

3 **Hide the bricks** and pump with a flat rock or a piece of slate. Choose plants that thrive with their roots permanently underwater and place them at the levels in which they grow best. The plants will hide the pump power cord.

4 **Fill the bowl** with water and plug in the pump. Add rocks to the bowl as desired, comparing the sound of the water falling on them with the sound of it falling directly into the pool. Be sure to replace water as it evaporates, so that the pump is always underwater. If you're adding fish, see "Introducing Fish" on page 167.

Serene Spill Fountain

A spill fountain requires no more than a watertight container of your choice with a larger watertight reservoir beneath it. Although large ceramic urns are often used for spill fountains, consider other interesting variations such as the piece of granite, with a natural bowl, used here. Whatever you use for the container will need a hole in its bottom for the tubing. Drill one if necessary.

1 Choose a reservoir 3 inches wider in diameter than the container. A half-barrel liner from a home improvement store works well. Dig a hole to the depth and breadth of the reservoir plus 2 inches. Put down 2 inches of sand and then settle the reservoir in place. Check for level and backfill around the sides.

2 Position the pump in the bottom of the reservoir and connect the tubing to it. Place a cinder block next to the pump to support the fountain bowl, first drilling a hole for the tubing to enter the block. Also cut a hole for the tubing in a piece of wire mesh that is 6 inches wider than the diameter of the reservoir. Fold back the sharp edges around the hole to protect the tubing. Run the tubing up through the hole in the cinder block and the wire mesh.

3 Run the tubing through the hole in the container, being careful not to kink the tubing. Seal gaps around the container's hole with pure silicone caulk. When the caulk dries, the tubing can be cut flush with the interior.

4 Fold down the wire mesh around the reservoir and cover the mesh with colorful stones to hide it. Fill both reservoir and container with water and plug in the pump.

Wall Fountain

Although the traditional lion's head spewing water springs to mind when you picture a wall fountain, almost any item can be used to create this feature. It might be a sheet of clear or stained glass with water running down its face, a gnarled driftwood branch with small containers mounted on it and water running from one to the next, or an old metal watering can with water pouring from its spout. Whatever you choose to hang on the wall, the components are always the same: a basin containing a submersible pump, tubing from the pump to the fountain spout, and water falling back to the basin.

Because wall fountains are often quite heavy, a strong support is recommended. A lag screw drilled into a wall stud is best, but finding the stud may take some effort. A stud sensor works on interior walls, but not on the stucco-covered exterior wall where this fountain was installed. If there is an outlet on either side of the wall, remove the cover plate to determine on which side of the stud the electrical box is mounted. Measure from the center of that stud to find a stud in the area where you want to hang the wall fountain: Studs are 1½ inches wide and are placed either 16 or 24 inches on center (measured from the center of one stud to the center of the next). Drill a tiny hole to confirm that you have found the stud, then attach the lag screw as described in Step 1.

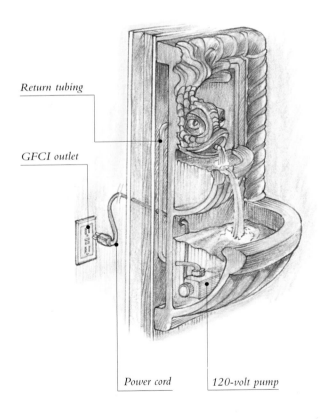

Return tubing

GFCI outlet

Power cord *120-volt pump*

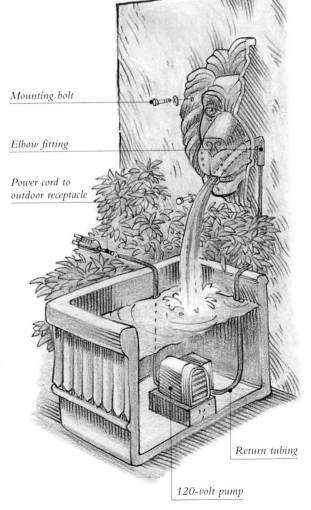

Mounting bolt

Elbow fitting

Power cord to outdoor receptacle

Return tubing

120-volt pump

1 **When you've located** a stud from which to hang the fountain, drill a ¼-inch hole through the siding at a slight downward angle into the stud. The angle will ensure that the fountain does not slip off its support. Using a wrench, turn a 4-inch-long, ⅜-inch-diameter lag screw into the hole until about an inch protrudes from the wall.

2 **Place the pump** in the bottom of the basin and connect the tubing from it to the fountain spout. The pump's cord can be covered later with decorative rocks or plants.

3 **Pumps generally have** power cords 10 feet long, which should reach the nearest outlet. However, in this case there was no outlet nearby, so the power cord had to be inserted through a hole in the stucco wall to an interior receptacle in the garage. Rather than drill a large hole to accommodate the plug, the plug was snipped off the cord with wire cutters. The cord was then taped to a straightened coat hanger and pushed through the small hole in the wall. Then the end of the cord was stripped back about half an inch and its wires were attached to a replacement plug, commonly available in hardware stores.

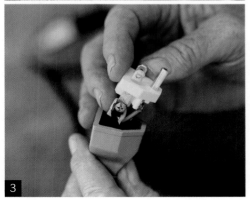

4 **The musical sounds** of falling water from the finished fountain, mounted here along a covered entryway to the house, provide a sense of coolness on hot summer days. This fountain was installed with a small 120-volt pump, but a low-voltage pump and transformer would do the job equally well. If your local supplier does not carry low-voltage pumps, you can order one on-line or from a catalog.

Freestanding Fountain

One of the easiest ways to enhance a yard or patio is with a freestanding fountain. Home supply centers often carry a selection, but you will find a wider array of choices in a shop that specializes in water gardens.

Freestanding fountains have a water reservoir containing a submersible pump that operates the fountain. Pumps may be either low voltage (see page 60) or main voltage (operating on household current). The low-voltage option is by far the easier and safer choice. You only need a simple transformer that steps down 120-volt power to a safe 12 volts and enough low-voltage

wire to reach the fountain. The transformer itself plugs into a 120-volt outlet, which if outdoors must be protected by a GFCI (ground fault circuit interrupter; see page 51). If you can't find a low-voltage pump locally, you can order one on-line or from a catalog.

Consider adding one or two underwater low-voltage lights for the fountain pool. This patio fountain is operated using a low-voltage system that includes two transformers, wiring, a pump, and an underwater light (the light requires a separate transformer because it needs to run only at night).

This three-part freestanding fountain includes a base, a basin, and a simple spill fountain. Hidden inside the hollow pedestal under the spill fountain, a small low-voltage pump recirculates the water.

1 **Mount the transformers** on a wall or a wood stake placed beside the house near a 120-volt outlet. Transformers simply hang from a screw, but keep them at least 12 inches above ground level. The larger transformer with a timer shown here is for the fountain pump; the smaller one is for the submersible light. Run the pump and light cords at the fountain to the transformers near the house. Some low-voltage cords come with simple

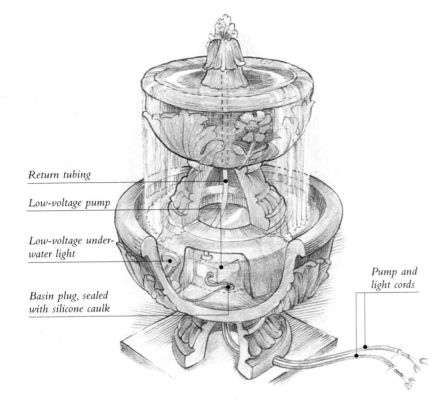

Return tubing

Low-voltage pump

Low-voltage under-
water light

Basin plug, sealed
with silicone caulk

Pump and
light cords

U-shaped connectors that slip under the contact screws on the transformers. If yours doesn't, strip about half an inch of insulation from the end of these wires. Loosen the contact screws on the transformers, wrap the wires you've exposed under the screws, and tighten.

2 **When low-voltage wiring** has to cross a lawn, it can be buried without significantly disturbing the sod. Using a taut length of twine to guide you, cut a 5-inch-deep slot in the sod with a square-tipped shovel. Push the handle away from you to widen the cut as you work. When the cut is completed, press the wire down into the slot with a stick. Simply press the sod back together with your foot, and the cut disappears.

3 **Position the pump** and the light where you want them in the fountain bowl, then run their cords down through the hole provided and down the base to the ground. Low-voltage pumps and lights usually come with an electrical cord and connector, but the patio fountain is often far from the outlet and transformers, as in this case. The solution is to splice in an extra length of wire. Cut off the connector and strip the cords' insulation back about an inch. Do the same with the new wire. You can make the connection watertight with heat-shrink electrical tubing, available in most hardware or home supply stores. Just slip a piece of shrink tubing over each of the wires to be joined, twist the exposed wires tightly together, and wrap the junction with black electrical tape. Slide the shrink tubing back over the taped area and heat it with a match or lighter until it pulls tightly around the connection. Now connect the wires at the end of this extended cord to the transformer.

4 **After checking** that the fountain is level, seal the wiring hole in the bottom of the basin with a special rubber plug, generally available where fountains are sold. These plugs, which come in various sizes, are slit on one side to accept wiring in their center. Slip the light and pump wires into the plug, press the plug into the hole in the basin, and then seal around it with pure silicone caulk. After connecting the tubing from the pump to your fountain, fill the basin and plug the transformers into the GFCI-protected outlet. If the pump does not begin operating immediately, check the setting on the transformer's timer.

Rigid-Liner Pond

Rigid-liner, or preformed, ponds are relatively easy to install. You can opt for just one, or several can be grouped together; on sloping ground, they can be connected with spillways, with a submersible pump installed in the lowest one to carry water back to the top. For a more natural look, and to protect the material from damage by sunlight, liner edges should always be concealed.

Rigid liners are available from home or pond supply stores in a variety of sizes and styles. They are usually made of cast polyethylene, polypropylene, or fiberglass. Most are about 4 to 6 feet long and 18 to 24 inches deep. The forms often have interior shelves, or "benches," built in that allow you to place plants at different levels. Fish can be added as well if you install a pump to keep the water aerated. (Rigid liners may not be suitable for koi, however, because of their relatively shallow depth.)

Before settling on a site for your pond, review pages 20–45, "Planning and Design," to be sure you've chosen the optimal location and considered all the relevant factors. And remember to call your local public utility companies before making your final decision, to ensure that there are no buried gas or water lines in the way (see page 50).

Once you've decided on the best site, you'll need an accurate outline of the pond shell to guide your excavation. If the shell is a symmetrical shape, you can simply turn the liner upside down and then trace its outline with landscaper's spray paint, but if you try this with an irregular shape, you will end up with the mirror image of what you wanted. Two ways to outline odd shapes are shown on the facing page.

A simple rigid liner, like the one forming the pond below, is available at most home supply centers. Set into the ground and edged with rocks, it is home to both water garden plants and a few small goldfish.

OUTLINING IRREGULAR-SHAPED POOLS

With the shell upright, extend a straight length of wood down from the rim at intervals and mark the points with landscaper's spray paint. When you remove the shell, you can connect the dots.

Paper bag template

Make a template using taped-together grocery bags. With the shell upside down, trace its outline on bags and cut away the excess. Remove the shell and flip over the paper template to get the correct version; then spray-paint around it.

If your shell has benches formed within it for water plants, your excavation will be more complicated. Digging the hole to fit the preformed shell requires some careful measuring so that both the benches and the bottom rest on firm earth. It may be helpful to make templates of the size and shape of the benches, so you can check your work in progress. Be prepared to try the shell in the hole several times, making various adjustments as you go.

If you plan on having a pump and fountain in the pond, make all the necessary electrical connections when you dig the hole but before you install the shell. If you're using 120-volt household current, the wire must be buried in electrical conduit. The receptacle must also be GFCI protected (see page 51), enclosed in a weatherproof outlet box, and located at least 10 feet from the water feature. Installing a low-voltage system, as described on pages 78–79, is much easier. Although low-voltage pumps are not widely available in stores, they can be ordered on-line or from catalogs.

Project continues >

1 **After choosing** your pond site, remove any sod and level the ground in an area at least 3 feet beyond the shell's rim. This will give you room to work. If necessary, use one of the methods shown on page 81 to trace the outline of your pond on the ground. Now you're ready to dig. You will want to make the hole about 2 inches larger all around than the shell; this allows you to maneuver it when you try it out in the hole. The 2-inch border will eventually be back-filled with sand to protect the shell from rocks and tough roots.

2 **Excavate the center** portion to its full depth first; then place the shell in the hole and trace the shelf outlines where they leave impressions in the dirt. Measure the depths of each of the shelves and dig to those points. A pointed shovel is ideal for the digging, but a square-tipped shovel will make it much easier to flatten the bottom and the shelves. If the shell has tapered sides, match the slope as closely as you can while you dig. Once you have an approximate fit, remove another 2 inches

from the bottom and the shelves; check them for level and then add that much sand to them, tamping it well. The sand will help you level the shell as well as protect it from any protrusions. Make sure the rim is flush with the ground.

3 **Check for level** in all directions, once the shell is in place. Rock it back and forth to adjust it. If the shell doesn't settle on the level, remove it and add more sand on the low side. The shell must be level, or the high side will be unattractively noticeable and will also be exposed to the sun's deteriorating ultraviolet rays. Now you can begin—very slowly—filling the shell with water while backfilling around it with sand. Do not let the water get higher than the sand, or it will distort the shell. Pack the sand down with a 2-by-4 as you add it. Keep a level across the shell to ensure that it does not shift during the filling process.

4 **Edging gives** your pond that special touch. Among the most attractive and easiest edgings to install are flat, smooth rocks that appear to have been shaped by water. Using the square-tipped shovel, flatten the ground around the installed shell, sloping the soil slightly away from the pond so that rainwater will not run into the shell, carrying dirt with it. Place the rocks around the pond perimeter so that their ends hang

over the edge by about 2 inches. This not only gives a nice shadow effect, but it also protects the shell from ultraviolet rays. If you add a second layer, offset the stones so the joints do not line up one above another, and set them back an inch or two from the edge.

Flexible-Liner Pond

For sheer versatility, there is no method of constructing a pond that can beat the flexible-liner option. It allows you to make the pond any size, shape, or style you want. Although it lends itself well to formal, geometric shapes, the flexible-liner method really shines when you envision a pond that appears to have been formed naturally, with curves that mimic those found in the wild. A particular advantage that the flexible liner has over rigid-shell, concrete, or masonry-block construction is that you can weave the shape around existing structures or mature plantings in your yard, causing less disturbance and certainly less relocation work. Your choices for placement expand further when you realize you can design different segments of a single pond linked by a narrower "waist" between them, perhaps connected by a waterfall or spanned by a small footbridge. Before settling on a style and layout for your flexible-liner pond, look over pages 20–45, "Planning and Design," to be sure you've considered all the limiting factors and taken advantage of all the possible options.

Added to the flexible liner's versatility is its ease of installation. Unlike the rigid-shell liner, which requires that you match your excavation precisely to

The advantage of a flexible-liner pond is that it can be formed to virtually any shape you want and positioned to flow around the natural contours of your landscape. Waterfalls and outdoor lighting are further enhancements.

BOULDER-RIMMED POND

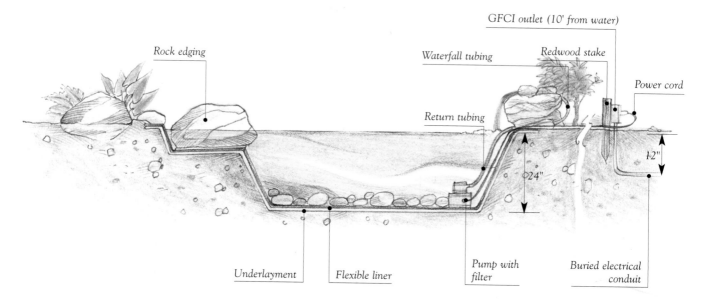

GFCI outlet (10' from water)

Rock edging

Waterfall tubing

Redwood stake

Power cord

Return tubing

24"

12"

Underlayment

Flexible liner

Pump with filter

Buried electrical conduit

DRAINAGE FOR A SLOPING SITE

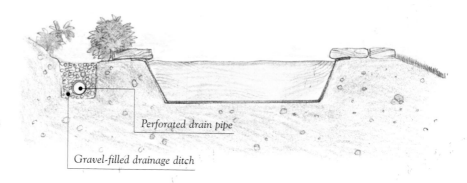

Perforated drain pipe

Gravel-filled drainage ditch

its shape, this method is more forgiving: the liner will cover a multitude of do-it-yourselfer sins. Today's 45-mil EPDM (ethylene propylene diene monomer) liner material is a flexible synthetic rubber that is resistant to ultraviolet rays and an improvement on earlier sheets of PVC, which tore easily and deteriorated when exposed to direct sunlight. EPDM comes in rolls up to 20 feet wide and 100 feet long. It can be solvent-welded together for larger ponds (but this is not recommended, because leaks can develop at the seam). Although it's tough, always protect it further with an underlayment.

For this project, there is a medium-sized pond with a natural shape and modest waterfall at one end (see facing page). Shelves were added at a depth of 12 inches to accommodate a selection of marginal plants (for examples see pages 144–153). Had we chosen to rim the pond with partially submerged boulders instead of flagstone edging, a shallower shelf would have been needed all around, as shown at the top of this page. And had our pond been sited on a slight to moderate slope, we would have added a swale, or ditch, on the high side, with perforated PVC pipe buried in it to divert runoff away from the pond (see the illustration immediately above). One person can do most of the work involved in this project, but it goes much faster and easier with two; at a minimum, you will probably need help when spreading the underlayment and liner.

Project continues >

1 Lay out several shapes with a garden hose until you find the one that both pleases you and conforms best to the surrounding elements—trees, garden plantings, or rock outcroppings. Allow plenty of time for this stage (several days to a week), sketching and photographing each outline so that you will remember it. As each proposed outline is laid out, look at it from several different angles; if possible, view it from a second story or other overhead perspective. A curving, irregular pond looks most natural; if you can, avoid sharp bends or corners, which are more difficult to fit the liner over.

2 Mark the outline with landscaper's spray paint once you are satisfied with the shape. (Sand or other substances can also be used.) Don't just scratch the outline in exposed earth; it may be obliterated before you begin digging.

3 Dig up and relocate any plants you want to keep that are within the outline. At the same time, be sure to clear and level a space a few feet wider than the pond perimeter so you have room to pile dirt, maneuver wheelbarrows, drag the underlayment and liner into place, and position the edging.

You will need two shovels: a round-tipped one for most of the digging, and a square-tipped one to level the plant benches and the bottom. Depending on your soil, you may also need a mattock or a steel pry bar to remove rocks.

4 **Excavate 12 inches** and then stop and mark out any plant benches that you would like to include. A piece of rope or wire will allow you to outline the shape, which you can then spray-paint, as shown here. You can make the shelves around the pond slightly different heights and widths to suit the needs of different plants; see page 31 for guidance as well as the descriptions of marginal plants on pages 144–153. You'll want to slope the benches slightly toward the pond wall to lend stability to any plant containers.

5 **Continue to dig,** sloping the sides backward at an angle of 60 to 80 degrees. As you work, verify that the pond's perimeter is all on the same level. With a smaller pond, you can do this by placing a level on a 2-by-4 set on edge spanning the excavation. (For holes too large for a 2-by-4 to span, see page 53.) Build up the low side of the rim with tamped dirt or remove soil on the high side. It is important that the excavation be level or the liner will be unattractively evident on the high side after you fill the pond.

Project continues >

4

5

6 Double-check for any sharp rocks or roots when the excavation is complete and the bottom is level. If the soil is rocky, pad the bottom with old carpet or carpet pad or add a protective layer of evenly smoothed sand. Alternatively, a high-quality underlayment material can be purchased where you buy the liner. The object of such protections is to keep roots and rocks from tearing the liner, either as it is being installed or later, when it's weighted with water. Fit the underlayment carefully around corners and over benches, using rocks to hold it in place temporarily. Now get some helpers to assist you in unrolling the liner and fitting it within the excavation.

7 Begin to fill the pond with water. The weight of the water will help the liner conform to the pond outline for a better fit. Working from inside, smooth the liner as much as possible and crease it as needed around curves and corners. In most cases, rocks or plants will eventually hide the liner and algae will obscure the folds. If you want to add a rock lining, begin stacking the rock from the bottom up the sides before filling. Fix rocks that won't stay in place with mortar, pure silicone caulk, or black expanding foam. (The latter two can be found at pond supply stores.) Mix large rocks, gravel, and some sand on the bottom for a more natural look. When you're finished, pump out the dirty water and resume filling.

8 Start adding the rock edging once the liner is in place and the pond is filled. If you're using flat rocks, as shown here, extend them about 2 inches over the lip of the pond. This not only hides the liner but also further protects it from ultraviolet rays. If you add more courses of flat rock, offset each stone so that the joints are not aligned. If you are using boulders, place them on a wide shelf excavated about 6 inches deep around the perimeter so that they appear to be rising from the water, as shown on page 85. Trim off any liner that extends beyond the edging.

9 **A simple waterfall** can be built with stacked rocks that conceal a hidden water supply tube from the pond pump. Run the tubing up behind the first course, leaving plenty of extra length for adjustments. Then stack the rocks for your waterfall and run water over them with a hose until you get the effect you like. Once the rocks are arranged to your liking, stack them permanently by adding mortar or pure silicone caulk between layers to stabilize the configuration.

10 **Two waterfalls** can flow simultaneously from each side of the rocks, as shown on page 84. To arrange this dual flow, the clear vinyl tube from the pump has a T-fitting at the end that sends the water in two directions. To secure this more elaborate arrangement, fasten the tubing to a stake with cable ties . A few well-placed plants will hide the plumbing.

MIXING MORTAR

For smaller masonry projects, use ready-mix mortar available in home supply centers. Empty a bag of dry mortar into a wheelbarrow, reserving some so that if you inadvertently make the mix too runny, which will weaken it, you can add more dry mortar. Slowly add water while continually turning the mix with a hoe or square-tipped shovel. Mix the mortar until all dry spots have disappeared and it is the consistency of toothpaste. Two 60-pound bags should be enough to lay the stones around this pond.

Simple Concrete Pond

If a diamond is forever, so is a concrete pond. Or nearly so. Once installed, it can be removed only with a jackhammer—so before you decide on one, make sure you want it and be sure where you want it. On the other hand, a good concrete pond will require little or no maintenance and will last for decades.

Like the flexible-liner pond, a concrete pond has the advantage of taking any shape you like. Although building one involves digging and concrete work, it is really not complex. And you can save both time and effort by mixing your concrete in a rented mixer.

1 **A conveniently** sized concrete pond is 6 to 8 feet long, 4 to 5 feet wide, and 2 feet deep. After using a hose or rope to lay out the shape, mark the outline with landscaper's spray paint (see page 86). Dig the sides 4 inches larger than your outline to allow for the 4-inch-thick concrete layer. As you dig down, slope the sides at no more than a 30-degree angle so that the concrete will adhere without slipping. Dig the base 8 inches deeper than the finished bottom will be; add 4 inches of gravel to support the 4 inches of concrete to come. Tamp down the gravel base and the soil on the sides firmly with the end of a 4-by-4 post or other suitable tool.

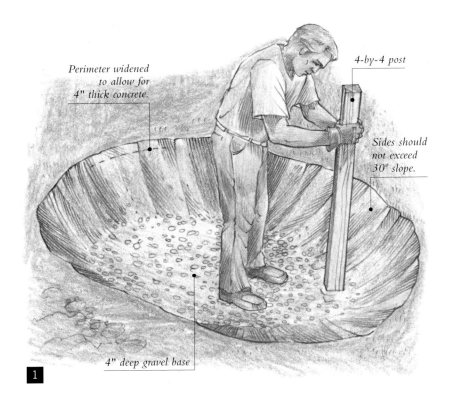

Perimeter widened to allow for 4" thick concrete.

4-by-4 post

Sides should not exceed 30° slope.

4" deep gravel base

1

Working with Concrete

If you've never worked with concrete before, here are a few pointers to help you along.

Concrete, including the ready-mix variety, is a mixture of Portland cement, sand, and gravel, with water added. Cement powder can irritate your eyes, lungs, and skin, so it's best to wear gloves, a dust mask, and eye protection when you work with it.

When mixing relatively large amounts of concrete, it is faster and easier to rent a concrete mixer for the job, even if you're using ready-mix bags. If you're making your own from scratch, use 1 part cement, 3 parts sand, and 3 parts gravel. Have tools, materials, and helpers in place ahead of time; make batches small enough to use before the concrete becomes too stiff to work—in 30 to 60 minutes, depending on the weather.

When mixing, follow the proportions of water to dry ingredients listed on the bag. Add a small amount of water at a time and mix it in thoroughly before adding more. The final mix should be the consistency of toothpaste. If your concrete batch is overly wet and runny, add more dry mix and continue mixing until it thickens to the proper consistency.

2 **After excavating** the pond, bend a length of 6-inch mesh reinforcing wire to fit in the hole and up the sides. Cut the wire along the edges as needed so you can fold it for a better fit. Once it's fitted, attach dobies underneath it. (Dobies are 2-inch-square concrete blocks with wires inset in them. Available in home supply centers, they are used to keep reinforcing wire or bars off the ground and suspended in the middle of the concrete pour.)

3 **To judge** the exact depth of the concrete as you shovel it, cut about a dozen 2-by-2 stakes 12 inches long. Drive them into the soil at 2-foot intervals, and then measure 4 inches from the soil surface and mark that point clearly on each stake. That will provide your concrete depth guide as you cover the bottom and sides.

4 **Keep the concrete** mix on the stiff side so it will stay put as you position it around the sides. Work first within the excavation to spread concrete over most of the bottom. When you can't stand on the bottom anymore, work from boards placed across the hole. Work the concrete evenly up the sides. When it reaches the 4-inch mark on a stake, remove the stake and fill its hole with concrete. The dobies will normally support the wire, but if you see some wire pressed against the soil, pull it up with a claw hammer.

Project continues >

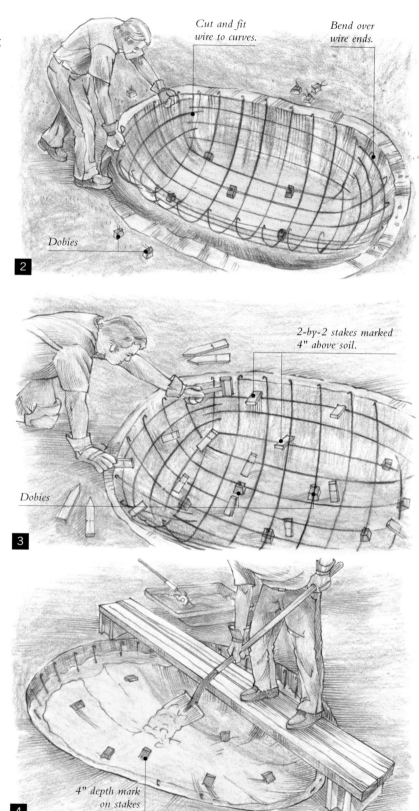

Cut and fit wire to curves.

Bend over wire ends.

Dobies

2

2-by-2 stakes marked 4" above soil.

Dobies

3

4" depth mark on stakes

4

5 **When all** the concrete is in place, smooth it with a wood float. If you want a polished surface, wait until the sheen of water that will appear on the concrete has evaporated and then go over it again with a steel trowel. (The concrete should be just hard enough for you to leave a thumbprint in it when you begin this step.) When you are finished, cover the concrete with plastic sheeting, weight down the edges, and let it cure for three days.

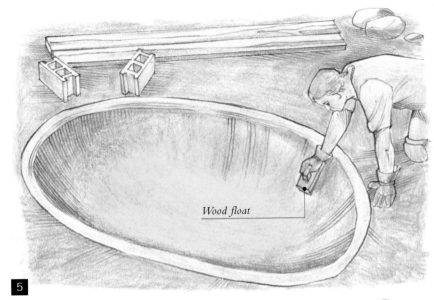

Wood float

5

6 **After** the concrete has cured, mortar an edging of your choice around the perimeter (see page 89 for instructions on mixing mortar). Using smooth stones will give the pond a more rustic appearance; brick will have a more formal look.

If your edging material is wider than the 4-inch concrete rim, prepare a packed-gravel base behind the rim to support it. Spread 1 inch of mortar over the gravel and the rim; set the edging in the mortar.

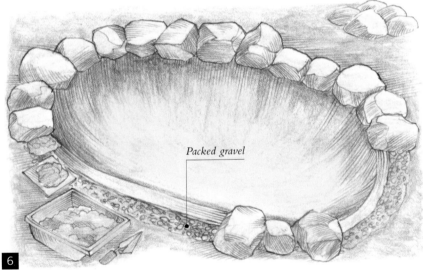

Packed gravel

6

CONCRETE AND FISH

The water in new concrete ponds is highly alkaline. This high pH level must be corrected before fish are introduced. Although alkalinity can be reduced by washing, filling, and draining the pond five or six times, a faster solution is to coat the concrete with a water-based epoxy paint, available at pond supply outlets and home supply centers. Prepare the concrete for painting by first scrubbing it with a mixture of one part muriatic acid and two parts water. Always add the acid to the water, never the reverse, and use a nonmetallic bucket. Wearing eye protection, scrub the surface with a long-handled brush until it's a uniformly gray color. Then rinse and drain the pond. When the surface is dry, paint it according to the manufacturer's instructions.

Raised Masonry-Block Pond

A raised pond is ideal for a courtyard or large patio. Its rim provides an inviting place to sit while watching fish move through the shadows beneath the lily pads. And because the pond is closer to eye level, there is less reflection on the water to disrupt your view. Although raised ponds can also be built with poured concrete, masonry-block ponds let you work in stages. You need only lay up a few courses at a time, rather than completing the whole pour at once, and there is far less concrete to mix. However, using this method limits you to square and rectangular shapes.

Masonry blocks are typically made of concrete, cinder, or pumice. The standard block is 8 inches wide and high, and 16 inches long. (These are "nominal" dimensions; they are all actually ⅜ inch less, which allows for the mortar joints.) The blocks are open inside except for a center divider, or web. Whatever type of block you choose, your masonry-block pond will require a footing to support it unless you are building on an existing concrete slab. Once the planning stage is complete and a practice run dry-laid, the whole structure can go together fairly quickly. There is no need to waterproof the blocks, because the water is all contained in a flexible EDPM liner (see page 85). When you are finished, the masonry-block exterior can be painted, stuccoed, tiled, or faced with brick or stone veneer.

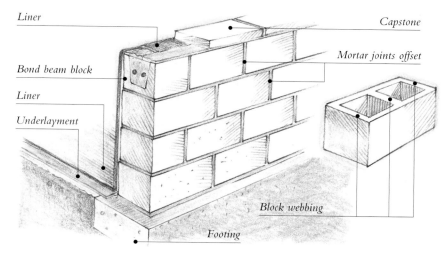

Liner
Bond beam block
Liner
Underlayment
Footing
Capstone
Mortar joints offset
Block webbing

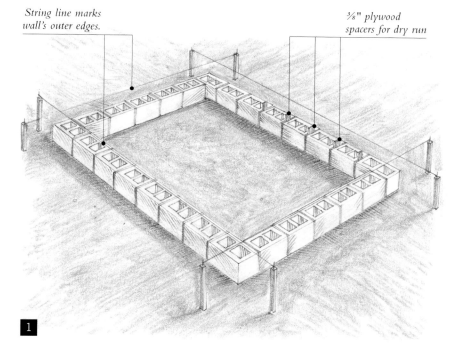

String line marks wall's outer edges.

⅜" plywood spacers for dry run

1 **Dry-lay one course** of blocks around the proposed perimeter, inserting pieces of ⅜-inch plywood between blocks to allow for the mortar joints. Adjust the spacing to accommodate whole blocks, so you don't need to cut any. Use a framing square to get the corners fairly close to 90-degree angles. To lay out the footing that will support these blocks, drive stakes at each end of one of the dry-laid perimeter walls. Drive small nails in the center of the stake tops and connect them with mason's twine.

Project continues >

2 **Form exact** right angles for the other walls using the 3-4-5 method. Measure 3 feet from point A toward point B and mark the twine at that juncture with a piece of tape. On a piece of twine running between A and C, mark the 4-foot point. Now move the A-C line in or out until the measurement between the 3-foot mark and the 4-foot mark equals 5 feet. The angle is then square. Continue around the perimeter in this manner. Double-check your work by carefully measuring the diagonals. If they're equal, the outline is square.

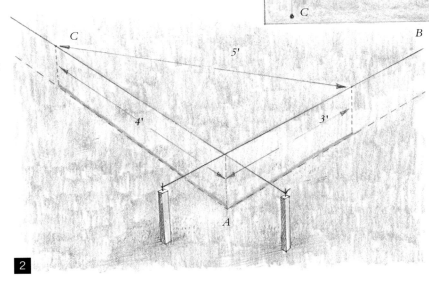

3 **Mark the ground** beneath the twine with landscaper's spray paint or sand and remove the twine and all the blocks. Begin to build the footing by digging a ditch 12 inches deep (or, in harsh-climate areas, to below the frost line). The ditch should be about 3 inches wider on each side than the concrete blocks, or as wide as local codes require.

To level the footing, drive stakes every 3 feet in the center of the footing ditch until they're approximately even with the ground surface. Place a level on top of the stakes and work your way around the footing ditch, tapping the stakes down until all are the same height. You're going to pour the concrete just to the tops of these stakes, leaving them in the footing.

4 **Lay reinforcing bar,** or rebar, in place before the concrete is poured: Lay pieces of scrap wood across the ditch and suspend ⅜-inch rebar from wires tied around the scrap wood. Hang one piece 3 inches above the bottom and the second one 3 inches down from the top. Where one length of rebar joins another, overlap them by 15 inches and wire them together. Pour the concrete flush with the tops of the stakes and smooth it with a steel trowel or wood float; let it cure.

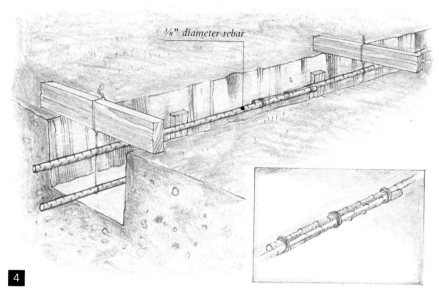

⅜" diameter rebar

5 **Snap chalk lines** on top of the footing about 2 inches in from the perimeter, to serve as a guide that won't be covered with mortar when setting the blocks. To prepare the mortar, see page 89. You will need roughly one 80-pound sack of mortar for every 27 blocks. Starting at a corner, spread a 1-inch-thick layer of mortar on the footing, long enough for three or four blocks. Press the first block down until there is a ½-inch layer of mortar beneath it. Check carefully that it is perfectly level. Spread mortar on the end of the next block and set it in place, maintaining a ⅜-inch mortar joint. Repeat the process for three or four blocks in the other direction, checking for level as you go.

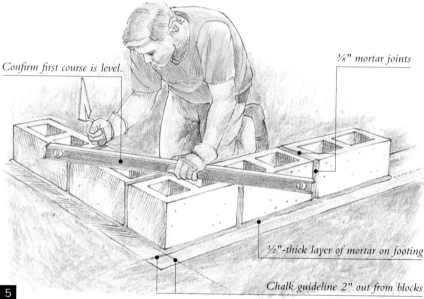

Confirm first course is level.

⅜" mortar joints

½"-thick layer of mortar on footing

Chalk guideline 2" out from blocks

Project continues >

6 **Construct leads,** or partial courses, at all four corners. Lay the first block of the second course in the alternate direction so that it overlaps half of the bottom block. This will ensure that the vertical joints will be staggered. Once you have corner leads, stretch mason's twine from line blocks aligned with the top edge of a course from one end block to the other. Using a line level, check for level frequently and adjust blocks immediately if necessary. As you move up each course, use a level to check that the wall is plumb, or vertical. Make adjustments by tapping the blocks with the trowel handle.

7 **When installing** the last block, or closure block, spread mortar over the lower block's webs and on both ends of the closure block; then slide it down and settle it into place. Scrape away any excess mortar.

Smooth and compress the mortar in all joints with a joint-ing tool as you work, before any concrete hardens.

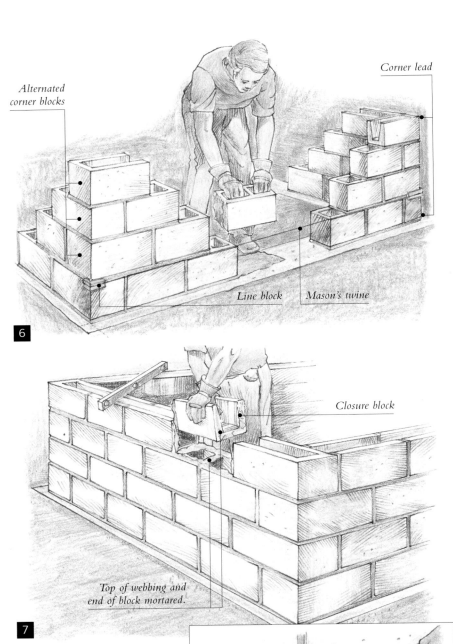

Alternated corner blocks

Corner lead

Line block   *Mason's twine*

6

Closure block

Top of webbing and end of block mortared.

7

Smooth and press with jointing tool.

8 **Use bond beam blocks** for the top course to add strength to the structure. These are U-shaped blocks with an open top, a solid bottom, and no webs. Lay this block as you did the others, half-fill with mortar, and then place two lengths of ⅜-inch-diameter reinforcing bars side by side inside the long U of the blocks. When you join one length of rebar to another, overlap the ends by 15 inches and wire them together. Continue to fill the bond beam blocks with concrete and smooth the top surface with a trowel. (Another way to form a bond beam is to fill the web cavities in the top course with concrete. To keep the concrete from falling through the cavities, first place a layer of roofing felt or fine screen over the course below.)

9 **Completely cover** the pond bottom with a protective underlayment—old carpet is excellent —and drape the EPDM liner across it, folding it carefully in the corners for a smooth fit. Secure the top of the liner in place by running a bead of pure silicone caulk along the inner edge of the top block before pressing down the liner. Trim the liner with scissors so that it extends no more than halfway across the top block. Run another bead of silicone on top of the liner and then mortar the flat cap blocks in place. Half of the cap block will bond to the top course and hold the liner in place. Let the mortar cure for two days and then fill the pond.

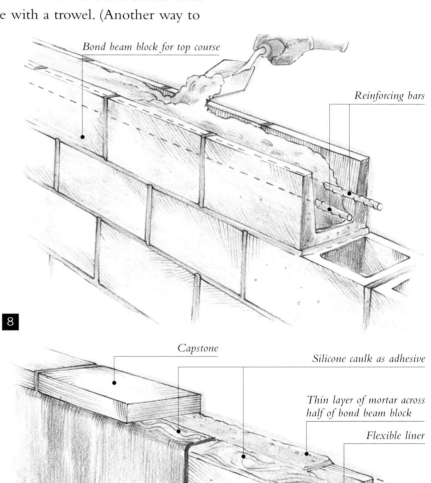

Bond beam block for top course

Reinforcing bars

8

Capstone

Silicone caulk as adhesive

Thin layer of mortar across half of bond beam block

Flexible liner

9

Raised Rigid-Liner Pond

Halfway between an in-ground pond and a raised one, a partially buried rigid liner is a quick and attractive way to add a water feature to your garden. It's a good solution when extremely rocky soil would make larger excavations daunting and you don't want to spend time pouring concrete or building with masonry blocks. For this project, the liner's plant benches rest at ground level, with just the lowest base section underground.

When your ground is hard and rocky, a raised rigid-liner pond is a good option. The base of the liner can be set as little as 3 or 4 inches into the ground. Rocks are then arranged up the sides of the liner to disguise it.

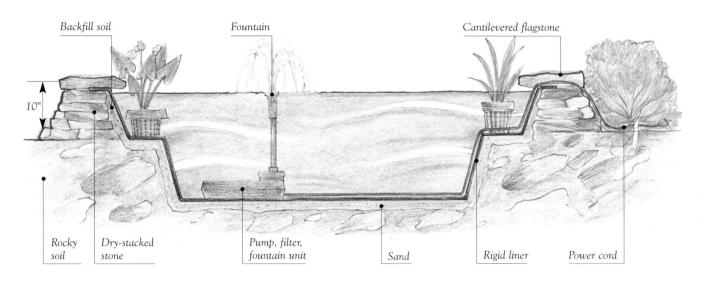

Backfill soil

Fountain

Cantilevered flagstone

10"

Rocky soil

Dry-stacked stone

Pump, filter, fountain unit

Sand

Rigid liner

Power cord

1 **Level the ground** and draw an outline of the liner to guide your digging (see pages 80–81.) Dig the hole to the depth of the liner's base section plus 3 inches for a sand layer. Dig the sides 2 inches wider all around the liner so that it can be backfilled with sand to support the structure. Add the sand in the bottom of the hole, tamping it evenly and thoroughly to keep the liner from settling under the weight of the water. The sand will protect the liner from roots and rocks as well as enable you to level the base of the hole.

2 **Place the liner** in the hole and carefully wiggle it around until it is level. You may need to lift out the liner and add or remove some sand to get it just right. Lay a level across the liner. Start filling the pond, double-checking the level frequently as you do.

Project continues >

3 **Backfill the sides** with sand or the excavated soil as the base section slowly fills with water. Tamp the soil or sand as you work, never letting the water rise higher than the backfill; otherwise, the weight of the water may distort the liner.

4 **Surround** the exposed upper portion of the liner with dry-stacked rocks, available from decorative-rock yards and some larger nurseries. Place the first layer of rocks a few inches away from the liner and then check to make sure this first layer is fairly level. Fill in the gap between the shell and the rocks with soil. Taper each rock layer closer to the liner, backfilling with soil to help support both the liner and the rock wall. Tamp the soil firmly as you go. Continue to slowly fill the pond as you work.

5 **Chip and break** stones, when necessary, for a better fit. Use a stonemason's hammer, as shown here. If a clean, straight edge is required, cut the stone with a circular saw that is equipped with a masonry blade. (Be sure to wear safety glasses for all cutting and chipping.)

6 **Build up** the rock layers until the surround is even with the top edge of the liner. Mortar a final course of rocks to the top layer, using the longest flat rocks that you have for this cap layer. The height of the capstones can be adjusted by adding more or less mortar underneath, to get them even. Allow them to hang over the lip of the liner by about 2 inches. This not only protects it from damaging ultraviolet rays, but also lends a greater sense of depth to the pond.

Stream and Waterfall

Contrary to what you might think, streams and waterfalls can be adapted to almost any terrain, steep or flat. Although sloping yards lend themselves most naturally to these features, flat ground can be built up convincingly. Many people mortar stones together near a backyard fence to simulate a small, rocky mountain with a waterfall at the top and a stream splashing down its face into a pond. Whatever your landscape, adding a stream and waterfall above a pond will not only make an attractive water feature but also add the pleasant language of water to mask everyday noises. Adding outdoor lighting, such as an underwater light behind the falls, allows you to enjoy the show at night as well as during the day.

Though most people enjoy the sounds of splashing and rushing water, not everyone appreciates them at the same volume. Fortunately, you can adjust the volume to suit your taste. For a booming waterfall, dig a deep and rather narrow hole into which the water can fall directly. For less boom and more splash, divert the falling water onto rocks. For a soothing whisper, avoid placing obstacles in the stream and instead direct the water over a sluiceway into a pond.

The stream-waterfall-pond combination shown in this project is fairly ambitious; see pages 88–89 if you want a simpler waterfall-pond arrangement. A waterfall

This homeowner chose a waterfall that tumbles into a deep pool for maximum sound effects. To see the entire project, turn to page 111.

and stream can also be constructed without including a pond. For a waterfall and stream alone, you need to build a buried reservoir at the bottom of the stream. A pump in this reservoir powers the water back up to the falls through a supply pipe. Water flows over

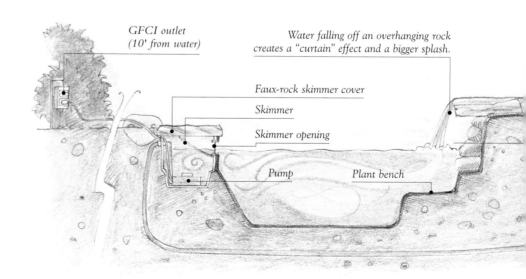

This stream and waterfall feature includes a pump that recirculates water from the pond at the base of the stream up to the waterfall reservoir at the top. The pump is located in the skimmer on the left side of the pond. Rocks and small falls in the stream add reality and soothing water sounds.

GFCI outlet
(10' from water)

Water falling off an overhanging rock creates a "curtain" effect and a bigger splash.

Faux-rock skimmer cover

Skimmer

Skimmer opening

Pump

Plant bench

the falls at the top, down the stream to the base, disappears into the ground through the rocks, and is recirculated. A special valve, called a check valve, prevents water in the pipe from draining back into the reservoir when the pump is turned off; thus, the reservoir need not be large enough to hold all the water in the system. The reservoir can easily be hidden with a variety of rocks and plants.

1 **When planning** just where to position the waterfall and stream, you will probably want to make it visible from inside the house as well as from a patio or deck. Other factors, discussed on pages 20–45, "Planning and Design," are equally important to consider. Streams and waterfalls are especially vulnerable to being dammed by falling leaves, so the presence of trees will weigh heavily in your choices. The sloping ground pictured here, leveling to a sitting area (not shown), is a natural location for this water feature.

Project continues >

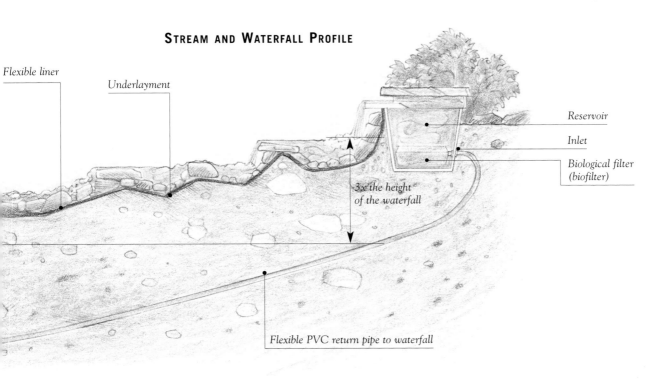

STREAM AND WATERFALL PROFILE

Flexible liner

Underlayment

Reservoir

Inlet

Biological filter (biofilter)

3x the height of the waterfall

Flexible PVC return pipe to waterfall

2 Experiment with the outline. After determining the start and end points of the stream, mark its approximate outline with ropes or hoses. Streambeds are usually 2 to 4 feet wide and 6 to 12 inches deep. The stream should ideally change direction and vary in width at several points. Add one or two small waterfalls to intensify the pleasing sounds of moving water; the pools they fall into will become reservoirs for still water when the falls are shut off. If you want to leave existing trees or large rocks in the stream's path, incorporate them into the design. A boulder, for instance, might appear to have forced the stream to change course naturally. If you don't have large rocks for this purpose, plan on bringing some in. Once you have decided on the parameters, mark the final shape with landscaper's spray paint.

3 A ready source of water for this project was a hose bib on the side of the house. Tapping into it was relatively painless, because no cutting was necessary. After shutting off the house water supply, the hose bib was removed and a 90-degree elbow installed on the end of the pipe. A gate valve was then installed by using two couplings (see page 57); an added T fitting allowed one outlet to feed the hose bib, the other the pond's water supply pipe. The gate valve lets the homeowner shut off water to the stream and waterfall for any maintenance and repairs without disrupting the household water supply. A nearby GFCI-protected 120-volt outlet supplied electrical power to the pump for the stream and waterfall. Electrical codes generally require that the outlet be at least 10 feet away from a water feature.

4 Prepare the waterfall reservoir base. The waterfall originates in a reservoir box set in a hole at the top of the stream. The depth of the excavation is directly related to the waterfall's height: it can be deep or shallow, depending on how high you want the falls to be. Many landscape contractors suggest that a waterfall be no higher than one-third of the difference between the pond surface (at the base of the stream) and the base of the waterfall. To ensure that it will not shift when filled with water, the box must be set on a solid foundation. After excavating to the desired depth for the reservoir, dig down another 6 inches and fill that with packed crushed rock to form the base.

5 Reservoirs commonly have factory-drilled holes in the rear wall, or bulkhead, where the water supply pipe is connected. After setting the reservoir in place, install the fittings for the supply pipe. Generally these are two threaded attachments that screw together, with a rubber gasket in between. Seal around the attachments with pure silicone caulk. Different manufacturers use different connections, but all include directions.

6 Dig out the ground in back of the reservoir for the water supply pipe. In this case, because there was limited room to work behind the reservoir, the 2-inch pipe was brought in from the side and then routed into the back of the reservoir through a 90-degree elbow. The pipe was then attached to the fitting in the bulkhead with PVC primer and glue. This pipe was later connected to the flexible PVC pipe, coming up from the pump, using a reducer coupling.

Project continues >

7 **To function properly,** the water-fall reservoir must be perfectly level from side to side but tipped forward slightly. (If the box is at all tilted to one side, the water will run to the low side of the spillway rather than forming an even sheet.) Use a 4-foot level to position the reservoir from side to side; then tilt it forward until the bubble is about a quarter of the way off center. Add or remove some of the crushed rock base to position the reservoir. Once it's properly placed, backfill around the reservoir with soil and pack it firmly as you proceed. To stabilize the box during this process, have someone stand in the reservoir. Check the level repeatedly to ensure that the reservoir does not move.

8 **In nature,** wide and shallow streambeds contain slow-moving water; swift water is seen in narrower and deeper channels. As you begin to dig, adjust the depth and width of the streambed to your terrain and your preferences. This homeowner wanted a considerable roar, so a 2-foot-deep pool was dug out directly under the falls. Smaller waterfalls and pools were added in the streambed to supplement the volume. The changing directions of the stream will add dynamism to the water feature. As you dig your stream, excavate a few deeper holes in the middle and along the sides. Later, you can fit larger rocks into these holes so that water will swirl around and over them.

9

9 **Water coursing** down a stream tends to flow up and over the banks at the inside of bends. This can cause erosion as well as a significant loss of water. Therefore, when excavating the streambed, dig down several extra inches inside the curves to help contain the water. For extra insurance, increase the height of the bank at those points with rocks and soil. Your banks may have to be adjusted after a few test runs. As well as placing rocks in different positions in the middle of the stream, you'll want to arrange some in a V shape, open at the bottom, to accelerate the water. Forming small dams with rocks will cause it to pool where you want to slow it down. Rapids pouring into calm, wide pools are common in rivers, and you can incorporate the same rhythms into your stream as you construct it.

10 **Like a pond,** a stream needs to be covered with a protective underlayment before you lay the liner. The underlayment, generally a synthetic matting material, can be purchased where you buy the liner, but old carpet or carpet pad works well, too. Some pond and stream builders suggest using layers of newspaper as an underlayment, but these tend to disintegrate in a few years, endangering the liner. The sole object of any underlayment is to keep the liner from tearing on exposed rocks and roots. The standard 45-mil EPDM liner (see page 85) often comes with a 20-year warranty and can be expected to last 50 years or more when properly installed.

Project continues >

10

11 **Fit the underlayment** across the streambed and up the sides. Press it carefully into any holes that have been dug out for large rocks and secure it temporarily with weights. As you work, add or remove soil as needed until the underlayment fits smoothly. If sharp rocks or roots cannot be removed from the streambed, cushion those spots further before installing the liner. Now spread the liner. At the top of the stream, where the waterfall reservoir is positioned, leave ample amounts of liner; this will later be fitted against the reservoir. Starting from the top, pull the liner across the streambed and then mold it to the excavated outline as you work your way down. All creases in the liner should fold down-slope; this makes it easier to fit rocks to the liner. Smooth and fold the liner with extra care at bends in the stream. Leave plenty of extra liner on both sides of the stream, so that you can build up the banks if needed.

12 **The skimmer is** a resin or fiberglass box with a windowlike opening in one side. The waterfall supply pump is placed in the skimmer, which filters out debris before sending clean water up to the waterfall. The skimmer is placed at the edge of the pond so that about 1 inch of the opening is below water.

SKIMMER

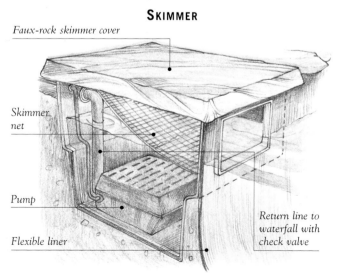

Faux-rock skimmer cover

Skimmer net

Pump

Flexible liner

Return line to waterfall with check valve

A skimmer, which collects floating debris, is useful in larger water features. A pump in its bottom draws in water through an opening near its top. The lower part of the opening should be about 1 inch below the surface of the water. The debris drawn in with the water is caught by a net in the skimmer.

DETERMINING THE WATER LEVEL

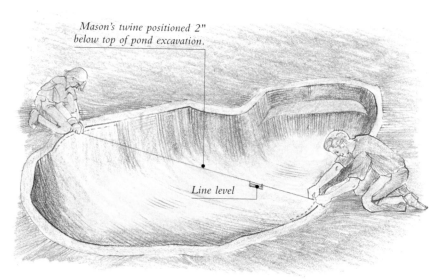

Mason's twine positioned 2"
below top of pond excavation.

Line level

To accurately position the skimmer so that the bottom of the opening will be 1 inch underwater, you must first determine what the pond's water level will be. Normally, a pond's surface should be about 2 inches below the top of the excavation. Working with a helper, hold one end of a length of mason's twine 2 inches below grade. Using a line level on the tightly pulled twine, your helper will mark the water level around the pond every few feet. (A transit or laser level performs this task with even greater precision.) Measuring down from this point, excavate the edge for the skimmer, setting it on a base of packed crushed rock. Adjust the height by adding or removing some rock.

13 **The pump,** seen here at the bottom of the skimmer box, is connected on the discharge side to a check valve. This is essentially a flap inside the fitting that opens when water is pumped up to the waterfall but closes when the pump is turned off to prevent water from running back down the pipe and overflowing the pond.

14 **A 2-inch-diameter** flexible PVC pipe is connected from the pump in the skimmer box up to the waterfall reservoir. Depending on the most convenient route between the two locations, the supply pipe can be buried under the streambed or where it runs up the side of the falls, as in this case. To prevent accidental damage to the pipe, bury it at least a foot below grade and even deeper if future gardening and digging will be done near it.

Project continues >

13

15 **Pull the excess** liner that you left at the top of the stream up to the face of the reservoir. Leave ample slack, so that it is not stretched later when you fit and glue rocks against it and the reservoir. Many reservoir boxes have a removable snout on the front that forms the waterfall spillway. If yours does, remove the screws holding the snout, cover the area under it with pure silicone caulk, and press the liner against the reservoir. Use an awl or nail to poke openings through the liner where the screw holes are located and replace the snout. The liner should extend out at least 2 feet on each side of the reservoir to prevent splashed water from escaping.

16 **After attaching** the liner to the reservoir, begin installing rocks up and around the box to hide it and the liner. For the most natural appearance, begin by placing the largest rocks on each side of the reservoir to frame it. From there, build up and around the box with a variety of small to large rocks. In this case, the homeowner had a large supply of flat rocks and chose to mingle them with the bigger stones. The stones can be attached to one another and the liner with mortar, pure silicone caulk, or black expanding foam. The caulk and foam are highly adhesive and are sold at pond supply stores. The foam is also used to fill gaps between large rocks. (After the foam has been sprayed, you can disguise it by pressing gravel and sand into it.)

17 **Many landscape** contractors prefer to use mortar when building a stream or waterfall, because mortar will hold stone to stone better than silicone does. To disguise mortar between rocks you can add color to it, such as the black tint used here.

18 Waterfall reservoirs often come with a faux rock piece that is glued to the plastic snout forming the spillway. An actual stone for the waterfall lip, however, will give the falls a significantly more realistic appearance. Here a wide, flat rock is fitted to the snout and fixed in place with pure silicone caulk. If a suitably flat stone such as slate or sandstone is not native to your area, check with rock supply firms. Slate and sandstone can be cut to fit with a circular saw equipped with a diamond-tipped blade—or, more slowly, with a masonry blade. Be sure to wear eye protection while cutting. How far out the stone extends will also determine the type of falls you have. For a straight plunge into a pool below, extend the lip out until it is directly over the water. If you want the water to splash down and over rocks supporting the waterfall, which will be quieter than the direct plunge, allow the water to fall on rocks at the top of the stream rather than into a pool.

19 Add a variety of plants to give your project that final touch and to soften the rocky outline. Grasses and ferns that naturally thrive beside streams will generally look good in a residential setting, though what you plant will probably be influenced by your local climate and native plants. On the other hand, you may wish to add an underground sprinkler or drip watering system to support lush tropical plants regardless of where you live. Consult pages 136–153 for information on plants well suited to water features.

18

19

Installing a pond, stream, and waterfall requires planning and hard work, but the results are well worth it. Such a water feature will instantly become the focal point in your yard, a delightful retreat where you and your friends can gather to enjoy the sights and sounds of moving water.

Dry Creekbed

Dry creekbeds comprised of variably sized smooth rocks suggest the presence of water without even the minimal maintenance demands of other water features. These "creeks" work well in desert regions, but serve a real function in any climate when placed in wet areas to direct seasonal runoff. To control seasonal flooding, you can install perforated plastic pipe in a gravel-filled ditch to direct the underground water to the dry creekbed, which in turn can carry the water to a storm sewer or natural runoff area.

The trick to making a pile of rocks look like a streambed is to arrange them along a slight depression; more importantly, construct the creekbed with stones that appear to have been worn smooth by centuries of flowing water. Some should be round, others flat—mix large and small together, just as they would naturally occur in an actual stream.

A dry creekbed provides the pleasant suggestion of a stream without the maintenance of a real water feature. Moreover, it can double as drainage to direct seasonal runoff away from the house.

1 **Lay out** the proposed streambed in a natural drainage area if at all possible. Use two hoses or landscaper's spray paint to adjust the streambed outline so that it seems to meander naturally. Make some parts wide and others narrow, as in a real stream. With a shovel, dig out a shallow depression within the streambed confines. Keep the sides concave, not vertical.

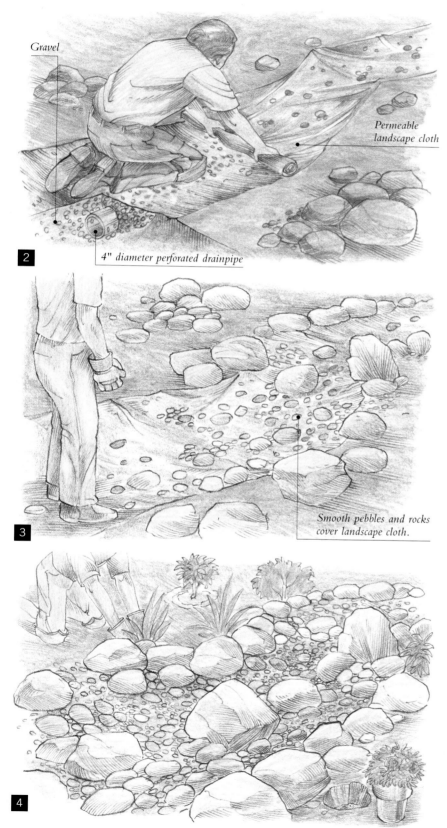

Gravel

Permeable
landscape cloth

4" diameter perforated drainpipe

Smooth pebbles and rocks
cover landscape cloth.

2 **Line the ditch** with landscape cloth to prevent weeds from growing among the rocks. Fold and pleat the cloth as needed where the stream curves, narrows, and widens. Then pour smooth pebbles over the cloth, covering it completely. (If extra drainage is required, bury a 4-inch diameter drainpipe in gravel before laying the landscape cloth.)

3 **Place larger rocks** along the edges, with a few pushing into the stream's center. The smaller stones mostly go in the middle, positioned among the smooth pebbles. Be sure the stones do not line up in a regimented manner but are located naturally. Fill in gaps among the large rocks with smaller ones.

4 **Add plants** all along the sides of the streambed. Use plants native to your area—for example, mix tall grasses with lower flowering shrubs.

CHAPTER FIVE

Water Garden Plants

YOUR GARDENING POSSIBILITIES INSTANTLY EXPAND when you install a water feature. You can select fascinating plants that you have always dreamed of growing—from exquisite water lilies and lotuses to little floating plants that form colorful carpets on the pond surface and luxuriant species that flourish in shallow water at the edges of waterways. ❦ Like most other garden plants, these water lovers need care to look their best—but at least you don't have to worry about irrigation, for the most part. Some even derive their nutrients directly from the pond, relieving you of the task of feeding them. ❦ And what you do need to provide water garden plants is explained in this chapter. The types of plants and their functions in the water garden are described, along with advice on designing with them. Don't miss the plant encyclopedia at the end of the chapter, depicting many of the wonderful choices available to water gardeners.

Designing with Water Plants

You'll want to include a few plants that serve specialized functions, such as providing oxygen and helping reduce algae in the pond (see "Oxygenating Plants" on page 118). Beyond that, your goals should be pretty much the same as when you design any other kind of garden: to choose plants that will provide variety and interest throughout the year and to arrange them in a visually pleasing way.

PLANT SIZE

Before choosing a plant, consider whether its mature size will be right for your water garden. If you have a small pond, you don't want overly large plants to dwarf it. Big plants encircling a small pond obscure the water and make pond maintenance diffi-

cult. If you have a large pond, you want to avoid a preponderance of plants that are too diminutive for good effect. Generally, what works best for any garden, regardless of size, is a mix of heights and widths, as long as no plant is so big that it eclipses the water feature.

The plant encyclopedia beginning on page 136 gives mature sizes for many common water plants; you'll also find sizes stated in some aquatic nursery catalogs. And, of course, you can always ask a supplier about ultimate dimensions before buying a plant.

VARIETY AND CONTRAST

A pleasing combination of different plant shapes and textures provides much of the visual

interest in a water garden. You may choose from upright, round-headed, vase-shaped, sprawling, weeping, or spiky plants. There's also variety in foliage, from big bold leaves to smaller, more delicate and even feathery ones. There are many categories of leaf shape to choose from—for example, linear, oval, or arrow-shaped leaves.

Mix it up: look for vertical accents like taller grasses and rushes; low, spreading species like water hyssop *(Bacopa monnieri);* plants with big, dramatic foliage like umbrella plant *(Darmera peltata);* and plants with finely divided leaves like ferns.

COLOR
Flowers are the most obvious source of color. Some aquatic plants, like water lilies, lotuses, and irises—all of which bear showy flowers in a wide range of colors—are unparalleled in the impact they make. Other species may contribute more modest blooms in a single color, such as sunny yellow marsh marigold *(Caltha palustris)* or lavender blue pickerel weed *(Pontederia cordata).* Some plants have subtle blooms, like the brown sausagelike flowers of cattail *(Typha* spp.).

As flashy as flowers may be, don't forget the contribution of foliage color. Some plants feature variegated leaves—for example, *Houttuynia cordata* 'Chameleon', with its combination of green, cream, yellow, pink, and red. The green foliage of some water lily varieties is splotched with red, purple, or brown. Hosta leaf colors include various green shades, chartreuse, gray, and blue; some varieties are bordered or splashed with white, cream, yellow, or gray-green. Even among strictly green-leafed species, you'll find many shades of green that may be combined artistically.

LASTING APPEAL
Try to have something of interest happening in your garden from earliest spring through fall. For example, choose plants with different or overlapping bloom periods so that you see bursts of color throughout much of the growing season. If the blossoms of some of the species are scented, you'll add fragrance to your sources of enjoyment.

Including some evergreen plants, especially in wintry climates, is a good way to extend interest. These plants will give definition to the water garden when the other species are dormant or in winter storage.

SPECIALIZED WORKERS
Be sure to include aquatic plants that advance a pond's health; read about the important roles played by oxygenators and floating plants (see pages 118 and 120). In the section on floaters, you'll find advice for the maximum amount of water surface that those plants should cover.

Pickerel weed (Pontederia cordata), *an exceptionally cold-hardy marginal plant, contributes lavender blue flower spikes as well as handsome heart-shaped leaves.*

Plants in the Pond

Several categories of plants actually grow in the water: submerged oxygenators, floating plants (some rooted and others drifting freely), and marginal plants. Use all three types for a healthy, attractive pond.

OXYGENATING PLANTS

These submerged species contribute to the health of a pond in several ways. During daylight, when photosynthesis occurs, they take up carbon dioxide and release oxygen to other plants and to fish in the pond. You can often see tiny bubbles clinging to a submerged plant's foliage as evidence of its oxygenating power. At night, when photosynthesis shuts down, submerged plants consume oxygen.

By absorbing nutrients directly from the water, oxygenators help clean the pond and also slow down the growth of algae, which compete for those nutrients. Additionally, oxygenating plants provide natural hiding and spawning places for fish.

Underwater plants even contribute aesthetically to the pond when the water is viewed close up. Foliage undulating beneath the surface gives the pond an added dimension and makes it look more natural.

ABOVE: *The oxygenators submerged in this pond help keep the water clear, making it easier to view the fish. They thrive on the extra oxygen that these plants—and the waterfall—provide.*

LEFT: *This pond contains a healthy mix of aquatic vegetation: water lilies and other floating plants; marginal plants, including irises; and oxygenating plants submerged in the water.*

A GOOD BALANCE It's important to have the right number of submerged plants in your pond. Too few, and algae will prosper. Too many can clog the pond as well as rob fish of oxygen at night (see "Balancing the Water" on page 164).

Some common oxygenators include fanwort (*Cabomba* spp.), pondweeds (*Elodea* and *Potamogeton* spp.), and eel grass *(Vallisneria americana)*. They are usually sold in bunches held together with a metal clasp near the base. It's a good idea to choose several types of oxygenators, since their periods of active growth may vary. Also, you may find that certain species are better suited to your water conditions.

These rapid growers need occasional thinning to keep them from taking over a pond. They may become invasive if planted directly in the soil of earthen ponds. It's better to keep them in pots instead (see "Planting Oxygenators" on page 129). They prefer a depth of 1½ to 2 feet, but will grow in ponds as shallow as 10 inches or as deep as 4 feet.

Like other oxygenators, Canadian pondweed (Elodea canadensis)—*its tips just visible at the pond's surface—aerates the water in the daytime.*

PLANTING PROFILE

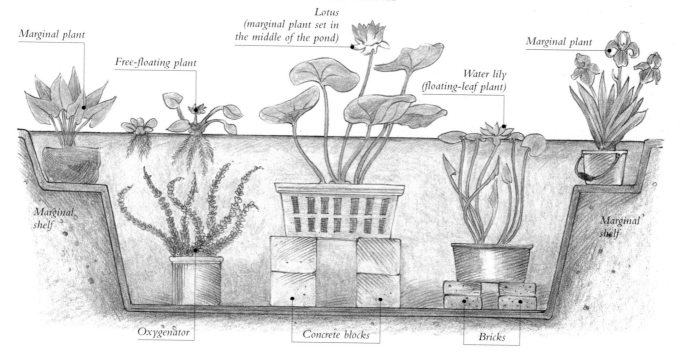

Marginal plant

Free-floating plant

Lotus (marginal plant set in the middle of the pond)

Water lily (floating-leaf plant)

Marginal plant

Marginal shelf

Marginal shelf

Oxygenator

Concrete blocks

Bricks

When you first glance at a pond, you may not realize that the plants are set at different levels in the water. To accommodate their individual depth requirements, place them on marginal shelves or on bricks, concrete blocks, flat rocks, or inverted pots.

FLOATING PLANTS

Two types of aquatic plants have floating leaves: free floaters, whose roots dangle in the water, and floating-leaf plants, which are rooted in soil. In addition to beautifying a pond, both types reduce algae growth by shading the water.

FREE-FLOATING PLANTS This small group of plants has hair-like roots that absorb nutrients directly from the water. True floaters add movement to the pond, shifting position in a breeze and subtly altering the appearance of the water surface.

These plants are sometimes likened to ground covers, because they quickly cover a

pond. Most can become invasive in mild-winter climates and consequently are banned in certain locales. Even if they're legal in your area, free-floating plants should be thinned regularly. You probably don't want them in a very large pond unless you have a way of removing excess plants.

Floating heart (Nymphoides peltata), a floating-leaf plant, is a relative of water lily and is sometimes substituted for it in very small ponds and tub gardens.

FLOATING-LEAF PLANTS These long-stemmed plants grow with their leaves floating on the water surface and their roots in soil at a deeper level of the pond. (Some water garden nurseries and pond suppliers list them as "deep-water plants" or "semi-floaters.") They thrive in calm waters, away from any splashing fountains or waterfalls.

Water lilies are the most widely grown floating-leaf plants; read more about them on the facing page.

This little plants-only pool features an assortment of pond plant types that covers most of the water and softens the look of the concrete.

How Much Cover?

Some people like open water, while others prefer a lot of plants in the pond. Before deciding on the number of floating plants you want, calculate the surface area of the water (see page 36). Too many plants will interfere with the exchange of gases and block sunlight from getting through to fish and oxygenating plants. Thus, floating plants should cover no more than one-third of the surface if the pond contains large fish. They can cover as much as one-half to three-quarters of the surface if there are small fish, or no fish at all, in the pond.

Water Lilies

These flamboyant floating-leaf plants are the reason many gardeners build ponds. Bearing exquisite blossoms over a long period, water lilies are the showpieces of any water garden. Even when the plant is out of bloom, the lily pads—the rounded, deeply notched floating leaves—are eye-catching.

The plants range from miniature, small-leafed varieties that cover about a square foot of pond surface to large species that may spread over 25 square feet. In some varieties, the leaves are colorfully spotted or blotched.

Water lily blossoms come in many sizes, shapes, and colors; several types bear a delightful fragrance. Although most water lilies need 5 or 6 hours of sun, certain varieties are shade tolerant, blooming with as little as 3 hours of direct sunlight.

Water lilies may be hardy or tropical (see below). To view some of the most popular varieties, turn to pages 138–141. For information on planting and propagating water lilies, see pages 129 and 131. Also note that koi can uproot and shred lilies, so you may want to choose other fish or plant the roots in baskets for protection.

HARDY VARIETIES Easy for beginners to grow, hardy types bloom in flushes throughout warm weather and go dormant

The beautiful blossoms of tropical water lilies stand prominently above the water while the leaves float on the surface.

in fall. They can overwinter in a deep pond.

Hardy varieties bloom in the daytime, holding their blossoms barely above the water surface. The color range includes white, yellow, orange, salmon, red, pink, and peach. Some varieties, called changeable water lilies, change blossom color as they mature—for example, turning from yellow to orange.

TROPICAL VARIETIES Since these water lilies grow best when outdoor temperatures are above 70°F/21°C, they shouldn't be set out too early in the growing season. They start to bloom a little later in summer than hardy

varieties do, but their bloom season extends longer, often until the first frost. Although the plants go dormant in winter, they should be brought indoors in all but the mildest climates.

This group tends to produce larger plants and larger, more fragrant blossoms than hardy kinds. The best tropicals bear up to three times as many flowers as hardy types do. Carried on stiff stalks well above the water surface, the flowers come in blues and purples in addition to the same hues as the hardy types. Most varieties show off their blossoms during the day, but some in the white-pink-red range are night bloomers.

MARGINAL PLANTS

In nature, these species are found along the edges of a pond or stream in shallow water (usually 1 to about 6 inches deep). Also known as emergent plants, they are rooted in the muddy bottom, with the lower portion of their stems submerged and their upper growth above water.

Most water gardeners, however, plant these species in pots that they set in the pond either on a built-in shelf or on bricks or other props (see the illustration on page 119).

A marginal plant need not be restricted to the edges of a pond. Some pondkeepers prop a single spectacular plant like a lotus in the middle of the pond as a showpiece. Others create the illusion of an island by grouping several plants in the center.

WHY MARGINALS? Because this category of plants is so diverse in size, form, and color, it lends a great deal of variety and interest to a water garden. Species are often chosen for their ornamental flowers or foliage, or for their height. While floating plants are specifically identified with water, marginal plants set at the edge of a pond help make a natural transition from the water to terrestrial plantings.

Marginal plants contribute to the water garden in other ways. They provide shelter for beneficial insects and for amphibians and other aquatic wildlife. Additionally, taller plants shade the water from the hot midday sun. And because marginal plants grow rapidly in water, they lend a pond a mature look quickly.

Heavenly Lotuses

A water lily relative, lotus (*Nelumbo* spp.) is a larger plant bearing its dramatic foliage and flowers above the water. Actually, the young leaves start out floating on the surface like lily pads, but sturdy leafstalks soon propel the foliage several inches to several feet above the water.

Lotus varieties vary in size from dwarf forms to giants with leaves 2 feet across, flowers up to 1 foot wide, and stems 6 feet above the water surface. Open only during the day, the fragrant blossoms come in white, cream, pink, red, and yellow. Although lotuses bloom for a shorter period in summer than do water lilies, they make up for that shortcoming by producing long-lasting, impressive woody seedpods perforated like huge saltshakers. After the petals drop, the seedpods are often harvested for dried flower arrangements.

The plants themselves are tough, holding up better than water lilies to koi damage. Although quite hardy, lotuses grow best in warm climates.

Majestic lotuses are sure to be the focal point of any water garden they occupy. Use tall, large-leafed forms like this only in ponds big enough to accommodate them.

MANY CHOICES Most marginal plants are soft-stemmed, nonwoody plants, including such popular choices as cattails *(Typha* spp.)*, irises, pickerel weed *(Pontederia cordata)*, arrowheads *(Sagittaria* spp.)*, water canna *(Thalia dealbata)*, and great bulrush *(Schoenoplectus tabernaemontani)*. Although some trees like willow and swamp cypress can grow in water, they are suited only to very large ponds, and their dropped leaves must be regularly skimmed from the water.

Many marginal species are described on pages 144–153 of the plant encyclopedia. Note in the descriptions that some of them can be used as either marginal plants or bog plants; they will grow in standing water as well as in wet soil and are difficult to categorize. (For information about bog plants, refer to pages 124–125.)

ABOVE: *Cattails are grown for their attractive narrow leaves and sausage-shaped flowerheads.*

CLOCKWISE FROM TOP LEFT: *Japanese iris, Siberian iris, blue flag, and yellow flag.*

INFINITE VARIETY

Like their forms, which range from tall and spiky to low and spreading, the foliage and flowers of marginal plants are extremely diverse—sometimes within a single plant type. For example, moisture-loving irises come in a range of heights, with either broad or narrow leaves, and with white, blue, lavender, purple, rose, red, pink, or yellow flowers. The most popular species for water gardens include Japanese iris *(I. ensata)*, *I. laevigata*, yellow flag *(I. pseud-acorus)*, blue flag *(I. versicolor)*, and Siberian and Louisiana irises (derived from several species).

LEFT: *Moist stream banks are ideal locations for a diverse mix of bog plants chosen for handsome foliage and colorful flowers.*

BELOW: *Vibrant, tiered blossoms of primrose (Primula) enliven a damp, shady spot bordering a pond.*

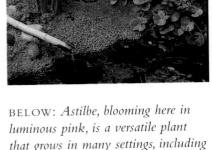

Plants Around the Pond

Bog and other moisture-loving plants grown just outside of the pond extend the "feel" of the water garden; they also visually link the aquatic plantings with terrestrial ones.

BOG PLANTS

True bog plants flourish in the wet—but not waterlogged—ground bordering most ponds and other waterways. They are often confused with marginal plants, but unlike them will not thrive if their roots are submerged in water.

Some marginal plants, however, will serve double duty: they'll grow in boggy conditions as well as in standing water. Because of this crossover in categories, marginal plants and bog plants are described in the encyclopedia in a combined grouping (you'll find it on pages 144–153).

Some species of bog plants, such as umbrella plant *(Darmera peltata),* are closely associated with water gardens, but others might just as easily be found elsewhere in your yard—for example, astilbe, hosta, and lilyturf (*Liriope* spp.). Many bog plants thrive in regular garden borders as long as they receive the proper amount of moisture.

BELOW: *Astilbe, blooming here in luminous pink, is a versatile plant that grows in many settings, including damp soil around a pond.*

FREESTANDING BOG

Rocks to disguise edges of liner

Boggy soil 12 in. deep

Pond liner pierced in spots to keep excess water from accumulating

2-in. layer of pea gravel

AN IMPORTANT ROLE Useful in concealing the edges of a pond, bog plants also make a water feature appear larger than it really is. And, just as marginal plants do, bog plants provide shelter for beneficial insects and wildlife such as frogs.

CREATING BOG PLANTINGS

The most common water garden bog is a freestanding permanent planting bed next to the pond that is lined with a flexible liner. (See more about making a bog garden on page 26.) You can use rocks to hide the edges of the liner, as shown in the illustration above, but gravel or a wood-based mulch will work just as well.

You may decide to connect the bog and the pond during construction by extending the liner over a shelf; you build the connected bog in the same way as a freestanding one, except you erect a rock dam to keep pond water from flooding the bog. Placing landscape fabric between the rocks and the boggy soil helps prevent soil from filtering into the pond.

A third option, for people short on space, is to create a mini-bog on an existing marginal shelf of a pond. As with the connected bog, you must dam it from the rest of the pond, using landscape fabric to prevent soil in the mini-bog from working its way into the pond water.

MINI-BOG ON A MARGINAL SHELF

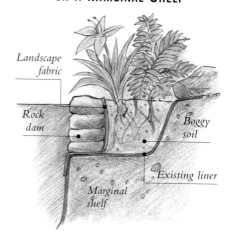

Landscape fabric

Rock dam

Boggy soil

Existing liner

Marginal shelf

Integrating the Design

To create a graceful transition between your water garden and the landscape around it, choose plant species that are compatible with the plantings in both areas.

TRANSITIONAL PLANTS

The role of these plants is to form a smooth progression from the water garden to neighboring beds and borders. Without some transition, the pond may look as if it has been plunked down in the middle of the yard without any regard for what's around it.

Here's how to tell if transitional plantings are effective: Not only do they seem appropriate near the pond plantings, but they look at home in your yard even when you block the water garden from your view.

WHAT KIND OF PLANTS? Your choice of transitional plants depends entirely on your pond plantings and those elsewhere in your yard. That in turn will hinge on where you live and your style of garden. As long as your selections are adapted to the climate and growing conditions and fit the look of your landscape, they're the right choices.

In a northeastern or coastal northwestern garden, try woodsy, moisture-loving plants whose lush appearance ties together the pond and other landscape plants. In the Midwest, you may feel that prairie natives are most appropriate for the transition. If you garden in the South, you can use coleus, weigela, perennial hibiscus, or other plants associated with gardens in that region.

In the arid Southwest, rather than having the pond blend seamlessly with the rest of the garden, you may want the water feature to look like an oasis. In this case, look for water-conserving but fairly luxuriant plants such as rosemary to connect the pond with plantings that become progressively more drought-tolerant the farther they are from the pond.

TRICKS OF THE TRADE Unity is that intangible quality that joins all parts of the landscape into a pleasing whole. In order to unify a landscape, garden designers repeat colors, shapes, or other elements.

Try using a few of the same kinds of plants in the water garden and elsewhere in the yard (for instance, irises or grasses). Or you can feature a distinct plant form (tall and spiky, for instance) or foliage type (such as arrow shaped) in both areas. Repeating a color, whether it appears in foliage or flowers, is a good way to tie everything together: designers often use silver or white as a unifier.

Color is used as a unifying element in this landscape. The yellow of the water lily blossoms is echoed in plantings on either side of the water feature and elsewhere in the yard.

Planting in the Pond

Water plants purchased at local nurseries or pond suppliers are sometimes suitably potted up and ready for placement in the water. If they're not, you'll have to get them ready for the pond, as you would any mail-order plants that arrive with bare roots or in very small shipping pots.

CONTAINERS

Most water gardeners plant in pots, even when it's possible to do otherwise. Not only do the pots restrain vigorous plants, but they simplify maintenance—you just lift the pots out when it's time to divide the plants or clean the pond.

STYLE Pond owners use all kinds of containers: plastic nursery pots, boxes constructed from rot-resistant wood (but not redwood, which can discolor the water), and even dishpans and other tubs.

Various types of containers that allow water and gases to circulate are made especially for aquatic plants. They include plastic baskets with lattice walls; some have perforations so small that soil won't escape, but others with larger openings must be lined to hold the soil in place. Tightly woven fabric pouches, which don't need lining, are also designed for aquatic plants.

SIZE AND SHAPE In general, try to choose larger containers over smaller ones, so long as you can pick them up when they're filled with wet soil. Large pots provide more growing room, and they're less likely to tip over. You may even want to plan on an extra-wide marginal shelf to hold big pots when constructing your pond.

Choose pots that are wider than they are tall for plants with horizontal growth habits or whose roots spread sideways, such as hardy water lilies, irises, and cattails (*Typha* spp.) Taller pots are appropriate for plants with an upright, clumping growth habit, such as rushes (*Juncus* spp.) and great bulrush (*Schoenoplectus tabernaemontani*).

SOIL

Special aquatic soil mixes are available, but most people use their own garden soil. The best type for water gardening is a heavy soil like a clay loam that is free of peat moss, manure, and other amendments that might float away or pollute the pond.

If your soil isn't suitable, buy an aquatic mix rather than one made for terrestrial plants. Most standard potting soils are too lightweight for water gardening; also, many of them contain fertilizer, which could foul the pond water.

LINING LATTICE WALLS

Baskets with openings big enough for soil to filter through require an extra step: you must first line the interior of the basket when planting. Water gardeners typically use a porous material like natural burlap or rot-resistant landscape fabric.

PLANTING MARGINALS

Carefully remove the marginal from the nursery pot.

Set the plant in soil so that its crown is exposed.

Add a layer of pea gravel, topping it off level with the plant crown.

Here, a marginal in a 4-inch pot is being transplanted into a larger pot made of porous, rot-resistant fabric. Many other types of pots could be used—for example, plastic mesh baskets—but fabric pouches don't need lining, they conform to the shape of the surface on which they are placed, and they have no sharp edges to harm fish.

PLANTING

Aquatic species are best planted while they are actively growing. You can do it anytime after spring growth begins, but wait until the risk of frost is over before potting up tropical plants. If you plant much after mid-summer in wintry climates, the plants may not become established before cold weather arrives; you have a longer window of opportunity in milder climates.

Remember, you can leave a plant in its original nursery pot if there is room for the plant's roots to grow, and if the soil mix is intended for aquatic use. If you decide that you must repot the plant, the illustrations on these pages will guide you.

TECHNIQUES Before placing any soil in the container, first line the interior if there are large holes that might allow the soil to escape (see "Lining Lattice Walls" on page 127). Fill the pot one-half to three-quarters full with moistened soil. To give a boost to heavy feeders like water lilies and lotuses, you can bury slow-release fertilizer tablets formulated for aquatic plants in the soil near the bottom of the container. While you're preparing the pot, be careful that the plant's roots do not dry out.

Plants that grow upright can be positioned in the middle of the pot. Those with horizontal growth habits or creeping roots should be placed at the edge of the container, with the growing point toward the center of the pot. Place the rhizome in the soil, carefully burying any attached roots.

Be sure to leave the plant's crown (where the stem meets the roots) sufficiently exposed so that you'll have room to add a topdressing to hold the soil in place. A typical topping is a ½- to 1-inch-thick layer of pea gravel (though koi owners often use larger stones like river rocks to discourage their fish from rooting around in the soil). When you're finished, the plant's crown should be level with the top of the stones. Water the potted plant thoroughly.

For more information on planting water lilies and oxygenating plants, see the facing page.

POTTING WATER LILIES

Solid-sided pots or fabric pouches are better containers for water lilies than those with perforated sides—the plants' aggressive roots tend to escape through the openings. A water lily container can be fairly shallow but should be wide—for example, 20 inches wide and 10 inches deep for large varieties and perhaps half those dimensions for miniatures. Although water lily leaves absorb nutrients directly from the water, the plants will benefit from slow-release fertilizer tablets buried in the soil near the bottom of the pot. When the water lily is planted, its crown should be exposed above the gravel topdressing.

HARDY WATER LILIES

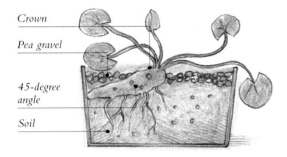

Crown

Pea gravel

45-degree angle

Soil

Hardy water lilies grow horizontally. Fill the pot partway with soil, then set the rhizome against the inside edge with the growing point angling upward about 45 degrees toward the center. Fill the pot to within 2 inches of the top and add a layer of gravel.

TROPICAL WATER LILIES

Crown

Pea gravel

Soil

Because a tropical water lily grows from a more vertical rhizome, set the plant upright in the center of a container nearly full of soil. Insert the rhizome into the soil and top-dress with gravel.

Planting Oxygenators

Submerged plants are often sold in bunches secured by a metal strip at the base. Most experts recommend one bunch per square foot of water surface. If your supplier sells them singly, ask how many you'll need for your pond.

You can simply toss these clasped bunches in the pond and let them sink. In a small pond, however, oxygenators are usually planted in pots to keep them from spreading too much and clogging the pond. Groups of up to eight bunches are commonly planted in a single pot (remember to remove the metal clasps first). It's also a good idea to pot up submerged plants for a koi pond, to shield them from the fish—you may even want to wrap the whole planting in bird netting for further protection.

You can pot oxygenators in gravel rather than soil, since the plants absorb nutrients through their leaves. Some species like eel grass (*Vallisneria americana*) are shallow rooters that spread by runners; they can be planted in shallow pots or trays.

LEFT: *Different types of marginal plants grow best at different water depths. You can set a potted plant on a shelf (if the pond contains one) or prop it up to get it to the recommended level.*

PLACEMENT OF PLANTS

It's important to place the pot at the plant's proper planting depth (measured from the top of the soil to the water surface). Some water garden suppliers specify the appropriate depth on the plant label; for the planting depths of many species, see the plant encyclopedia beginning on page 136.

To get plants to the correct level, set them on a marginal shelf or prop them on something sturdy and rot-proof like bricks, weathered or sealed concrete blocks, flat rocks, or inverted pots. You might start with a high stack of bricks for a small, newly potted plant and then adjust the height as the plant grows. If your pond contains large fish, choose heavy props that the fish can't knock over. Avoid props with jagged surfaces that could injure the fish.

You don't have to worry about positioning free-floating plants. Simply launch them in the water; their roots will settle to the proper level.

BELOW: *Even fairly tall containers can be used for tub gardens. You can prop up the potted plants inside the tub just as you would in a pond.*

Propagating Plants

The most common methods of reproducing water garden plants are by division and by stem cuttings. Spring is a good time to propagate most species in and around the pond.

DIVISION

Most water garden plants can be divided. You may decide to divide yours because you want more of them for yourself or for friends. But you're most likely to do it when a plant has outgrown its allotted space. Division will also rejuvenate plants whose growth is flagging.

Some species require division more often than others. There's no rule about how often to divide a given species: that will depend on the size of its container, the amount of direct sun it receives, whether it is fertilized, and the climate in which it is growing (plants get bigger in warmer areas with a longer growing season). The most vigorous growers may need division yearly, but slower growers may get by with division every three to five years.

You can often tell when a plant needs dividing simply by looking at it—for example, it's time to divide a water lily when its leaves stand up above the water and it produces very few flowers.

CLUMPING PLANTS Marginal and bog plants, including grasses and sedges, often grow from a network of fibrous roots (as opposed to a taproot). To divide them, pull them apart—either by hand or, in the case of large plants, with two spading forks positioned back-to-back for leverage. Discard the old growth in the center, since it's probably past its prime. Trim the healthy sections, rinse them off, and replant them.

RHIZOMES Some plants, such as water lilies and many irises, grow from an underground storage organ called a rhizome. With a sharp knife, cut the rhizome into two or more pieces, each having at least one growing point and some roots. Trim back the top growth and any long roots; then pot it up. (To see how to pot water lily rhizomes, turn to page 129.)

Two spading forks simplify the task of prying apart the roots of a large clump of daylilies (Hemerocallis).

CUTTINGS

Many oxygenators and some marginals reproduce well from cuttings. With sharp pruning shears, snip off a young, non-blooming shoot from the parent plant; then strip off its lower leaves. After dipping the base of the cutting into rooting hormone, insert it into a pot of moist potting soil, where it will soon form roots.

DIVIDING RHIZOMES

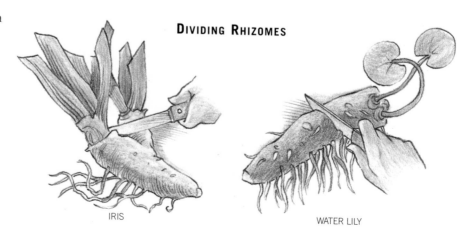

IRIS

WATER LILY

Plant Care

Water garden plants require routine care to thrive and look their best. While some aspects of care are the same as for a regular garden, others are unique to the watery environment in which these plants grow.

FERTILIZING

Feed plants outside the pond just as you would other garden plants, though there's no need to fertilize fast-growing bog plants. Likewise, marginal plants that grow quickly don't need extra nutrients—but lotuses and some other flowering marginals will bloom better when fed, as will water lilies.

Oxygenating and free-floating plants will take what they need directly from the pond water.

Fertilizers labeled for aquatic plants are safe for fish and other pond creatures; they're also low in nitrogen so that they don't foster algae growth. Most water gardeners choose slow-release tablets (lasting 30 to 45 days), pushed deep into the potting soil to prevent them from leaking into the water. Fertilize when planting; additionally, you may choose to feed blooming plants monthly from midspring to about a month before the first expected frost.

PRUNING

Routinely trim off any dead or diseased leaves and stems as well as spent flowers. The best way to remove yellowed water lily leaves is to snap them off at the base of the stem. Many water gardeners will wade into the pond to reach plants that are more than an arm's length away.

Be sure to prune back any plants whose growth is crowding into the pond or visually reducing its space. Even if they're not encroaching, grasses and sedges are among the perimeter plants that look better when cut back every year before new spring growth begins.

WEEDING, THINNING, AND DIVIDING

In addition to weeding, you'll need to restrain many aquatic plants. If free-floating plants spread too fast, they can take over just as weeds do—use a net or rake to skim off excess plants. You may also need to thin out oxygenators to keep them from clogging the pond. You can keep water lilies and many types of marginal plants in check by dividing them (see "Division" on page 131) and discarding or giving away the excess.

Because the material you remove may contain beneficial water creatures like tadpoles and dragonfly larvae, let the plant sit by the pond for a while to allow them to find their way back to the water.

Your water garden won't get out of hand if you tidy it on a regular basis rather than just once or twice a year. Pluck weeds whenever you notice them, and periodically thin out overgrown plants to keep some open space, as shown below.

PREPARING FOR WINTER

You may not need to protect your water plants in a mild climate. But if your pond is at risk of freezing, or if you're growing any plants too tender for your climate, take a little time to prepare for the cold weather ahead. Consult a water garden nursery or pond supplier if you're in doubt about how to handle a given species.

TROPICAL PLANTS Before the first expected frost, while they are actively growing and their leaves are a healthy color, bring tropical plants indoors to a warm spot that receives about 4 hours of sunlight daily. (Plant grow lights can be substituted for natural light.)

Marginal plants are often treated as well-watered houseplants. Alternatively, they can be kept immersed in leak-proof containers along with floating plants and oxygenators. The marginals need at least an inch of water above their root crowns (around 6 inches for oxygenating plants). Floating plants can simply float in the container.

You may overwinter cannas by drying out their rhizomes and storing them in a cool, dark, dry place. Water lilies may produce walnut-size offsets at the crown; these can be removed and stored in the same environment as the canna rhizomes.

HARDY PLANTS You can protect these plants in any of several ways, but first cut back their foliage when it begins to discolor or die. Here are some options for winter protection.

- Sink the plants to the bottom of the pond, as long as it's deep enough not to freeze solid. Cut back any tall oxygenating plants well below the water line, to prevent them from being frozen into the ice.
- Bury the plants, pots and all, in a garden bed. After draining the pots of excess water, set them into the ground, cover with several inches of soil, and top with mulch.
- Bring the plants indoors to a cool spot such as an unheated garage or basement. Leave them uncovered, and either water them regularly or keep them immersed in water, as you would tropical plants. Free-floating plants can be brought indoors or treated as annuals; where winters aren't too severe, they usually die back into winter buds that fall to the bottom of the pond and come to life in spring.

In this garden, tender plants were protected in winter while hardier types were left in place to brave the elements and resprout in spring.

Problems and Remedies

Water garden plants tend to suffer fewer problems, especially diseases, than other garden plants—but that doesn't mean they're immune from trouble. Be alert and take swift action once you spot a problem.

PREVENTION

Here are some ways to lessen the chances of trouble.

- Choose plants adapted to your climate. Don't rush tropical plants outdoors before it's warm enough.
- Check new plants for insects or diseased leaves before placing them in the water garden.
- Give plants the amount of sun or shade that they require.
- Fertilize plants that need it, but don't overdo it.
- Divide or thin out plants as needed.
- Keep the pond clear of debris that may harbor pests and diseases.
- Don't use pesticides that may kill beneficial insects, such as dragonflies, that feed on insect pests.

TREATMENT

When trouble does arise, choose the least toxic method of addressing it. Be especially leery of using chemicals if your pond contains fish. Refer to the chart on the facing page for some of the most common ailments and how to treat them.

PESTS Remove larger pests by hand. Hose off smaller ones, such as aphids, with a stream of water or submerge the infested growth to loosen the pests. Any fish in the pond will devour them. (If you weren't planning on having fish, consider keeping at least a few for pest patrol.)

If you want a more potent control than water, try the one least dangerous to organisms other than the target pest. Any commercial products you choose should be approved for use on aquatic plants.

Many water gardeners spray infested plants with oil to smother pests. Some use commercial products made from herbal oils. Others concoct their own, spritzing leaves with cooking spray or a solution of vegetable oil and dishwashing liquid (for example, 1 tablespoon of each in 2 cups of water). Any spray containing soap should be kept away from water containing fish. Regular horticultural oil can be used, but only outside the pond. In all cases, spray thoroughly because oil kills by contact; rinse the plant with water about an hour after spraying.

Bacillus thuringiensis (Bt) is a biological pesticide often used in water gardens. One formulation controls leaf-eating caterpillars. If you want butterflies in your garden, use *Bt* stintingly and only on plants hosting pest caterpillars. It's not very effective on the China mark moth caterpillar (see chart on facing page), which

Keeping the water free of fallen leaves and other debris not only beautifies the pond and makes it easier to see the fish, but it also helps you avoid many pests and diseases.

sandwiches itself between pieces of leaves. Another formulation of *Bt* works against mosquito larvae, though fish—especially mosquito fish—will also keep those pests under control (see page 163).

DISEASES Relatively few ailments strike plants in the water garden. The problems that do occur affect mainly water lilies. The controls for disease are always changing and new products come on the market as others are withdrawn. For this reason, it's a good idea to consult your Cooperative Extension Agent or an aquatic nursery or pond supplier to learn what's currently available.

SOME COMMON PLANT PROBLEMS

PROBLEM	VICTIM	DESCRIPTION	REMEDY
Aphids	Aquatic plants, especially water lilies	Tiny green, black, or brown insects are clustered on leaves; leaves are discolored or partly eaten.	Dislodge aphids by hosing them off or submerging plant; apply oil spray.
Aquatic leaf beetles	Aquatic plants, especially water lilies	Beetles (description varies according to species) lay eggs on leaves; their larvae eat the leaves.	Wipe eggs and larvae off leaves; fish (especially goldfish) will eat larvae.
China mark moth	Aquatic plants, especially water lilies	Brown-and-white moth lays eggs on plant; resulting larvae eat holes in the leaves. Sometimes called "sandwich man" because the caterpillar folds itself into a floating piece of foliage or debris.	Handpick larvae or hose them off; scoop out floating debris.
Fungus infections	Water lilies and some marginal plants, especially marsh marigold (*Caltha palustris*)	Water lily leaves have black spots or blackened and dry leaf edges. Marginal plants have mildewed leaves.	Cut off infected leaves; remove plant from pond and treat with fungicide.
Lack of nutrients; crowding	Water lilies, marginal plants	Leaves or flowers are smaller than normal, or there are no blooms at all on a flowering plant.	Fertilize plants; divide and repot them.
Leaf-mining midge	Water lilies	Upper surface of foliage has been tunneled; trails turn brown or black and then rot.	Pick off and destroy infested leaves.
Lily crown rot	Water lilies, particularly those recently planted or moved	Leaves are yellow; black spots start at leaf center and expand; crown is rotted.	Remove infected plant and destroy it.

Leaf-mining midge

Aquatic leaf beetle damage

Overcrowding

The aquatic luminaries in this pond are tropical water lilies, whose spectacular blossoms—hot pink and white in the varieties shown here—are held prominently above the water.

Plant Encyclopedia

The plants described on pages 138–153 are dependable ones that have passed muster with water gardeners. But many more possibilities exist, especially if you consider all the different varieties of some plants like water lilies. Experiment and see what works for you.

HOW THE ENCYCLOPEDIA WORKS

Most plants are grouped by category: oxygenating, free-floating, and floating-leaf plants have their own, while marginal and bog plants are combined in one. Water lilies are featured in special sections—one for hardy types and another for tropical ones. Be aware that suppliers may categorize certain plants differently, and that some may fit into more than one category.

Within each grouping, plants are listed alphabetically by their botanical name. Entries describing only one species are listed by both genus and species, as in the case of *Lobelia cardinalis*. Entries that aren't restricted to a single species are headed by the plant's genus name followed by the abbreviation for "species," such as *Iris* spp. (If you know a plant only by a common name, look for it in the index at the back of the book.)

Each entry provides a hardiness indicator (the minimum air temperature at which the species can survive), a description, planting tips, and the easiest method of propagation. All the plants are

perennial when grown in the right conditions. Note that "planting depth" for aquatic plants refers to underwater depth—the amount of water from the top of the soil to the pond surface.

FINDING THE PLANTS

Once you've decided on the plants you want, where will you get them? Local or mail-order nurseries and pond suppliers are good bets (see "Suppliers" on page 188). So are water gardening friends who may have divisions of plants to share. Collecting aquatic plants from the wild is usually prohibited.

It's fun to choose the plants yourself, but if you'd rather leave the decisions to someone else, consider one of the collections offered by some suppliers. There are different collections suited to different pond sizes (based on surface area). They typically include all the plants needed for a well-balanced pond.

This mass planting of primrose (Primula) occupies moist ground in a pondside bog garden. The tiered blooms in vivid shades of yellow, orange, and red create a blanket of color.

When shopping locally, try to choose vigorous, healthy-looking specimens with plump, well-hydrated stems. The plants should be free of any weeds and algae. Obtain them only when you're ready to put them in the pond.

If you're buying through the mail, place your order as early as possible, between October and April—water gardening suppliers are usually very busy during the growing season. Normally, you will be given some choice of when you want the plants delivered. Choose a date after the water garden is completed.

Ask about the size of the plants you will be receiving. Make sure the supplier will replace, free of charge, any plants damaged during delivery. Some suppliers ship plants in tiny plastic containers, which helps keep them moist; however, that additional weight can substantially increase shipping costs. Plants shipped bare-root are lighter and more economical, but they must be handled carefully to avoid damage. When the plants arrive, unpack them in a shady location and make sure they didn't become limp during shipping.

CAUTION

Certain species, especially among the free-floating plants, are considered invasive in mild-winter regions. Thus, depending on where you live, some of the plants given here may not be appropriate for you. Local nurseries and pond suppliers should know if a particular plant is prohibited in your area, even though a mail-order company in a colder region might ship the plant. You can consult with your Cooperative Extension Agent if you're in doubt about the status of a particular species.

Spice It Up with Diversity!

Many of the plants in this encyclopedia are available in different species and varieties. They may vary greatly—for example, have assorted forms, grow to different sizes, or differ in flower color or some other feature. The water lilies shown on pages 138–141 prove this point about diversity. Hostas are another good example. The many types have roundish to lance-shaped leaves that may be shiny or dull, with a smooth or puckered texture. Foliage hues include many green shades, chartreuse, gray, and blue; many are edged or blotched with a contrasting color.

This grouping of hostas includes white-edged 'Albo-marginata', which is a selection of H. fortunei *(front left); yellowish green 'Little Aurora' (front right); and blue 'Willy Nilly' (background).*

Hardy Water Lilies

'Attraction'

HARDINESS: To −40°F/−40°C. Become dormant in fall and reappear in spring. May overwinter in pond if rhizome remains below ice level.

FLOWERS: White, yellow, copper, pink, red; also changeable colors. Bloom throughout warm weather, during daytime only.

PLANTING: In water to 24 in. deep.

(Also see *Nymphaea* spp. on page 144.)

'Attraction'

DESCRIPTION: Big, slightly fragrant blooms with deep red inner petals, lighter outer petals. Shade tolerant.

SPREAD: 4–5 ft. wide

'Marliacea Chromatella'

'Colorado'

'Marliacea Chromatella' ('Chromatella')

DESCRIPTION: Fragrant yellow flowers. Young leaves blotched purple. Shade tolerant.

SPREAD: 3–5 ft. wide

'Gladstoniana'

'Colorado'

DESCRIPTION: Salmon flowers with slight scent. Some brown mottling on leaves.

SPREAD: 4–6 ft. wide

'Gladstoniana' ('Gladstone')

DESCRIPTION: Waxy white, slightly fragrant flowers. New leaves bronzy.

SPREAD: 5–8 ft. wide

'Pygmaea Helvola' ('Helvola')

DESCRIPTION: Miniature yellow flowers with slight scent. Leaves mottled purple. Shade tolerant.

SPREAD: 1–3 ft. wide

'Pygmaea Helvola'

'Gloriosa'

'Gloriosa'

DESCRIPTION: Bright red, slightly fragrant blooms. New leaves light purple. Shade tolerant.

SPREAD: 4–5 ft. wide

'Joey Tomocik'

'Pink Sensation'

'Pink Sensation'

DESCRIPTION: Silvery pink flowers with slight scent. New leaves purplish.

SPREAD: 4–5 ft. wide

'Joey Tomocik'

DESCRIPTION: Bright yellow, slightly scented blooms. Brown-flecked leaves. Shade tolerant.

SPREAD: 3–4 ft. wide

'Sultan'

DESCRIPTION: Cherry red blooms tipped and flecked with white. Slight scent.

SPREAD: 4–6 ft. wide

'Sunrise'

DESCRIPTION: Large, fragrant, canary yellow flowers.

SPREAD: 6–8 ft. wide

'Sunrise'

'Sultan'

Tropical Water Lilies

HARDINESS: To 30°F/−1°C. Remove from pond before first frost and keep indoors in a tub of water.

FLOWERS: White, yellow, copper, pink, red, purple, greenish blue, blue. Most varieties bloom in daytime, but some in white-pink-red color range flower at night. All bloom later in summer than hardy types but last longer, often until the first frost.

PLANTING: In water to 12 in. deep.

(Also see *Nymphaea* spp. on page 144.)

'Yellow Dazzler'

'Yellow Dazzler'

DESCRIPTION: Fragrant lemon yellow flowers in daytime. Some purple markings on leaves.

SPREAD: 6–8 ft. wide

'Daubenyana'

'Daubenyana' ('Dauben')

DESCRIPTION: Strongly fragrant lavender flowers in daytime. Shade tolerant. Slightly more cold hardy than other tropical varieties.

SPREAD: 3–7 ft. wide

'August Koch'

'August Koch'

DESCRIPTION: Fragrant lavender blue flowers in daytime. Shade tolerant.

SPREAD: 3–4 ft. wide

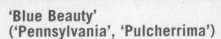

'Blue Beauty'

'Blue Beauty' ('Pennsylvania', 'Pulcherrima')

DESCRIPTION: Large, very fragrant, light blue flowers in daytime. Some brown markings on leaves.

SPREAD: 4–7 ft. wide

'Evelyn Randig'

'Evelyn Randig'

DESCRIPTION: Fragrant deep magenta flowers in daytime. Leaves mottled purple.

SPREAD: 5–7 ft. wide

'Red Flare'

'Red Flare'

DESCRIPTION: Big, fragrant, dark red flowers at night. Mahogany leaves.

SPREAD: 5–6 ft. wide

'St. Louis Gold'

'St. Louis Gold'

DESCRIPTION: Deep yellow day-time flowers with slightly sweet scent. New leaves bronzy.

SPREAD: 4–5 ft. wide

'Panama Pacific'

DESCRIPTION: Sweetly fragrant violet-purple flowers in daytime. Shade tolerant.

SPREAD: 4–6 ft. wide

'Panama Pacific'

'Sir Galahad'

'Sir Galahad'

DESCRIPTION: Large, very fragrant, bright white flowers at night.

SPREAD: 5–6 ft. wide

'Texas Shell Pink'

DESCRIPTION: Pale pink, spicy-scented flowers at night. Shade tolerant.

SPREAD: 5–6 ft. wide

'Albert Greenberg'

'Albert Greenberg'

DESCRIPTION: Fragrant blend of pink, yellow, and orange; blooms in daytime. Leaves speckled purple. Shade tolerant.

SPREAD: 5–8 ft. wide

'Texas Shell Pink'

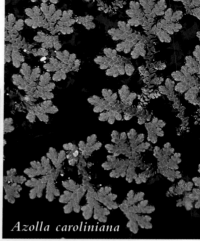

Cabomba caroliniana

Potamogeton

Azolla caroliniana

Elodea canadensis

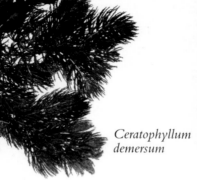

Vallisneria americana

Ceratophyllum demersum

OXYGENATING PLANTS

(See page 129 for general information on planting oxygenators.)

CABOMBA caroliniana
Fanwort

HARDINESS: To −10°F/−23°C

DESCRIPTION: Fan-shaped, feathery, bright green foliage. Small white flowers float on water in summer.

PLANTING: Best in warm, still water. Full sun.

PROPAGATION: Cuttings

CERATOPHYLLUM demersum
Hornwort, coontail

HARDINESS: To −10°F/−23°C

DESCRIPTION: Whorls of stiff, forked, dark green leaves on slender stems. Tiny white (male) and green (female) flowers bloom in leaf joints in summer.

PLANTING: Prefers sun but tolerates some shade.

PROPAGATION: Cuttings, floating small pieces of stem in water

ELODEA canadensis
Canadian pondweed

HARDINESS: To −30°F/−34°C

DESCRIPTION: Small, dark green leaves on brittle, threadlike, tangled stems. Tiny greenish white flowers in summer.

PLANTING: Thrives in cool water. Full sun.

PROPAGATION: Cuttings

POTAMOGETON spp.
Pondweed

HARDINESS: Some species to −20°F/−29°C

DESCRIPTION: Many species with translucent, seaweedlike leaves. Tiny flower spikes just above the water surface in summer.

PLANTING: Prefer sun but tolerate some shade.

PROPAGATION: Cuttings

VALLISNERIA americana
Eel grass

HARDINESS: To 20°F/−7°C

DESCRIPTION: Grassy clump of ribbonlike, bright green leaves. Long-stalked little flowers float on surface in summer.

PLANTING: Place in shallow, wide pot or tray to allow horizontal growth; new plants form along runners. Best in still water. Full sun.

PROPAGATION: Division

FREE-FLOATING PLANTS

(To plant all free floaters, simply place them on the water.)

AZOLLA caroliniana
Fairy moss

HARDINESS: To 0°F/−18°C

DESCRIPTION: Dime-size green fern with a single fine root. Turns red in bright sun or cool weather. A few plants quickly form dense mat.

PLANTING: Full sun or part shade.

PROPAGATION: In mild climates, generally self-propagating

Pistia stratiotes

Aponogeton distachyus

Hydrocharis
morsus-ranae

Salvinia minima

Hydrocleys nymphoides

Eichhornia
crassipes

EICHHORNIA crassipes
Water hyacinth

HARDINESS: To 10°F/−12°C

DESCRIPTION: Rounded, shiny green leaves to 5 in. across held just above the water, supported by air-filled stems. Showy, pale lavender blue flower spikes to 6 in. tall in warmer climates in summer. Foot-long feathery roots excellent spawning area for fish.

PLANTING: Full sun.

PROPAGATION: Division

HYDROCHARIS morsus-ranae
Frogbit

HARDINESS: To 0°F/−18°C

DESCRIPTION: Rounded, shiny green leaves, to 2 in. across, like little lily pads. Small, bowl-shaped white flowers with yellow centers in summer.

PLANTING: Prefers calm, shallow water. Full sun.

PROPAGATION: Division

PISTIA stratiotes
Water lettuce

HARDINESS: To 30°F/−1°C

DESCRIPTION: Velvety green 6-in. rosettes, like little heads of looseleaf lettuce. Can form a mat several feet wide by summer's end. Long, trailing roots turn from white to purple to black; good fish cover.

PLANTING: Prefers calm, shallow water. Needs midday shade in hot climates.

PROPAGATION: Division

SALVINIA minima
Water fern

HARDINESS: To 30°F/−1°C

DESCRIPTION: Fern with two rounded, stiffly hairy, ½-in. floating leaves like miniature lily pads; emerald green in shade but often brownish in full sun. Submerged, modified third leaf acts as a root.

PLANTING: Prefers still water. Full sun or part shade.

PROPAGATION: Division

FLOATING-LEAF PLANTS

APONOGETON distachyus
Water hawthorn

HARDINESS: To 23°F/−5°C

DESCRIPTION: Long-stemmed, strap-like, bright green leaves to 8 in. long. Fragrant white flowers 1¼ in. wide in two-branched clusters above the water from spring to early fall in cold climates, year-round in mild ones. May disappear in summer heat.

PLANTING: In water to 24 in. deep. Full sun or part shade.

PROPAGATION: Division

HYDROCLEYS nymphoides
Water poppy

HARDINESS: To 30°F/−1°C

DESCRIPTION: Long, trailing stems with heart-shaped, shiny, dark green, floating leaves to 3 in. long. Bowl-shaped 3-in. yellow flowers just above the water in summer.

PLANTING: In water to 12 in. deep, but prefers shallower water to 6 in. deep. Can also be grown as free-floating plant. Full sun.

PROPAGATION: Division

Marsilea mutica

Nymphaea 'Mrs. Martin E. Randig'

Nymphoides indica

Acorus calamus 'Variegatus'

Adiantum capillus-veneris

MARSILEA spp.
Water clover

HARDINESS: To −10°F/−23°C

DESCRIPTION: Ferns with foliage like that of four-leaf clovers.

PLANTING: In water to 12 in. deep. Also grow in moist soil, standing erect to 1 ft. tall. Can become invasive; best in pots. Sun or shade.

PROPAGATION: Division

NYMPHAEA spp.
Water lily

HARDINESS: Hardy types to −40°F/−40°C; tropical types to 30°F/−1°C

DESCRIPTION: Round leaves, deeply notched where stem is attached. Spectacular flowers—fragrant in many varieties—in white, yellow, copper, pink, red, blue, greenish blue, and purple.

PLANTING: In water to 24 in. deep for hardy types; to 12 in. deep for tropical types. Full sun (there are some shade-tolerant varieties).

PROPAGATION: Division
See varieties on pages 138–141.

NYMPHOIDES spp.
Water snowflake, floating heart

HARDINESS: Some species to −10°F/−23°C

DESCRIPTION: Most types have round leaves to about 3 in. across, sometimes mottled with brown. Small, fringed yellow or white flowers like little water lilies held above the water in summer.

PLANTING: In water to 24 in. deep. Full sun.

PROPAGATION: Division

MARGINAL AND BOG PLANTS

ACORUS spp.
Sweet flag

HARDINESS: Some species to −30°F/−34°C

SIZE: To 5 ft. tall, 2 ft. wide

DESCRIPTION: Grassy or strap-shaped leaves may be entirely green or striped with cream or white. Some dwarf forms are less than 1 ft. tall.

PLANTING: In moist, rich soil or in water to 6 in. deep (to 2 in. deep for dwarfs). Full sun or part shade.

PROPAGATION: Division

ADIANTUM spp.
Maidenhair fern

HARDINESS: Some species to −40°F/−40°C

SIZE: To 1½ ft. tall and wide

DESCRIPTION: Airy, finely cut, bright green fronds on thin, wiry, dark stems. Even cold-hardy types may die back in hard frosts.

PLANTING: In moist, rich soil. Part or full shade.

PROPAGATION: Division

ASARUM spp.
Wild ginger

HARDINESS: Some species to −50°F/−46°C

SIZE: To 6–10 in. tall, spreading by rhizomes

Asarum caudatum

Asclepias incarnata

Astilbe chinensis 'Pumila'

Bacopa monnieri

Butomus umbellatus

Caltha palustris

DESCRIPTION: Ground covers with heart-shaped green leaves (mottled in some forms). Small, usually brownish red spring flowers, mostly hidden beneath foliage.

PLANTING: In moist, rich soil. Part or full shade.

PROPAGATION: Division

ASCLEPIAS incarnata
Swamp milkweed

HARDINESS: To −40°F/−40°C

SIZE: To 2–4 ft. tall, 2 ft. wide

DESCRIPTION: Narrow, pointed green leaves to 6 in. long. Pinkish purple flowers in clusters to 4 in. across at stem tips in summer; 'Ice Ballet' has white blooms. All plant parts poisonous if ingested.

PLANTING: In moist soil. Full sun.

PROPAGATION: Seed, division

ASTILBE spp.
False spirea, meadowsweet

HARDINESS: To −30°F/−34°C (with good snow cover in coldest areas)

SIZE: To 3 ft. tall and wide

DESCRIPTION: Airy, plumelike flower clusters in white, pink, or red on slender stems above mound of lobed or toothed green leaves. Spring or summer bloom.

PLANTING: In moist, rich soil. Part shade; can take full sun in cool-summer climates.

PROPAGATION: Division

BACOPA monnieri
Water hyssop

HARDINESS: To 10°F/−12°C

SIZE: To 6 in. tall, spreading by rooting stems

DESCRIPTION: Sprawling ground cover with succulent, ¾-in. green leaves. Small white or pale blue flowers, spring into fall.

PLANTING: In moist soil at edge of slow-moving stream or pond. Will often extend shoots to float in water and send down long roots. Full sun or part shade.

PROPAGATION: Division

BUTOMUS umbellatus
Flowering rush

HARDINESS: To −20°F/−29°C

SIZE: To 4 ft. tall, 2 ft. wide

DESCRIPTION: Cup-shaped, rosy pink flowers in 4-in. clusters above grassy clump of dark green, twisted leaves in summer.

PLANTING: In moist soil or in water to 6 in. deep. Full sun or part shade. Won't tolerate hot-summer climates.

PROPAGATION: Division

CALTHA palustris
Marsh marigold

HARDINESS: To −30°F/−34°C

SIZE: To 2 ft. tall and wide

DESCRIPTION: Rounded, glossy green, toothed leaves 2–7 in. wide. Clusters of 2-in. bright yellow flowers in late winter, early spring. There are white-flowered and double-flowered forms.

PLANTING: In moist soil or in water to 6 in. deep. Full sun or part shade.

PROPAGATION: Seed, division

Carex elata 'Aurea'

Crinum americanum

Cyperus alternifolius

Canna 'Pretoria'

Colocasia esculenta

Darmera peltata

CANNA hybrids

HARDINESS: To 0°F/−18°C

SIZE: Variable: 1½ ft. tall and wide to 6 ft. tall, 3 ft. wide

DESCRIPTION: Large, lance-shaped leaves may be rich green, bronzy red, or variegated. Showy flower spikes in red, orange, yellow, pink, cream, white, or bicolors in summer, fall.

PLANTING: In moist, rich soil or in water to 6 in. deep. Best in sunny, hot spot.

PROPAGATION: Division

CAREX elata 'Aurea' ('Bowles Golden')
Bowles golden sedge

HARDINESS: To −20°F/−29°C

SIZE: To 2½ ft. tall, 1½ ft. wide

DESCRIPTION: Grasslike clump of bright yellow leaves with faint lengthwise green stripes. Brownish flower spikes in late spring, early summer.

PLANTING: In moist soil or in water to 4 in. deep. Leaf color most intense in full sun.

PROPAGATION: Division

COLOCASIA esculenta
Taro, elephant's ear

HARDINESS: To 20°F/−7°C

SIZE: To 7 ft. tall, 6 ft. wide

DESCRIPTION: Succulent stalks hold huge (to 3 ft. long), heart-shaped green leaves from spring through fall. There are forms with black or purple stalks and foliage.

PLANTING: In moist, rich soil or in water to 10 in. deep. Best in warm, filtered sun.

PROPAGATION: Division

CRINUM americanum
Bog lily, Florida swamp lily

HARDINESS: To 10°F/−12°C

SIZE: To 2½ ft. tall, 3 ft. wide

DESCRIPTION: Intensely fragrant, spidery white flowers in 5-in. clusters from spring to fall. Clump of straplike green foliage.

PLANTING: In moist, rich soil or in water to 6 in. deep. Set tops of bulb necks even with soil surface. Full sun or part shade.

PROPAGATION: Division

CYPERUS spp.
Umbrella grass, umbrella palm

HARDINESS: Some species to 20°F/−7°C

SIZE: To 1½–10 ft. tall, spreading by rhizomes

DESCRIPTION: Leafy green whorls atop triangular stems are umbrella-like. Choices include *C. alternifolius*, to 3 ft. tall, and *C. papyrus*, a dramatic accent 6–10 ft. tall.

PLANTING: In moist, rich soil or in water to 6 in. deep for larger species; for smaller species to 2 in. deep. Full sun or part shade.

PROPAGATION: Division

DARMERA peltata
Umbrella plant, Indian rhubarb

HARDINESS: To −20°F/−29°C

SIZE: To 6 ft. tall, 4–8 ft. wide

DESCRIPTION: Big clusters of pink flowers on leafless stems to 6 ft. in spring. Followed by 2–6-ft. stalks with shield-shaped green leaves to 2 ft. wide; foliage turns red in fall.

PLANTING: In moist soil. Part shade.

PROPAGATION: Division

Eleocharis
montevidensis

Dulichium
arundinaceum

Filipendula rubra
'Venusta'

Equisetum hyemale

Glyceria maxima
'Variegata'

DULICHIUM arundinaceum
Water bamboo, three-way sedge

HARDINESS: To −10°F/−23°C

SIZE: To 2–3 ft. tall, spreading
by rhizomes

DESCRIPTION: Narrow, bamboo-
like leaves arranged in three distinct
vertical rows along upper stems.

PLANTING: In moist soil or in
water to 4 in. deep. Invasive; best
in pots. Full sun or part shade.

PROPAGATION: Division

ELEOCHARIS spp.
Spike rush

HARDINESS: Some species to
−10°F/−23°C

SIZE: To 1–3 ft. tall, spreading by
rhizomes or runners

DESCRIPTION: Clumps of graceful,
green, grassy stems. *E. montevidensis*
grows to about 1 ft. tall. *E. dulcis*
(E. tuberosa), to 3 ft. tall, has edible
round tubers (Chinese water chest-
nuts) at ends of underground
runners.

PLANTING: In moist soil or in water
to 2 in. deep for *E. montevidensis;*
in water to 12 in. deep for *E. dulcis.*
Full sun or part shade.

PROPAGATION: Division

EQUISETUM spp.
Horsetail

HARDINESS: To −30°F/−34°C

SIZE: To 6 in.–4 ft. tall, spreading
by rhizomes

DESCRIPTION: Rigidly upright,
dark green hollow stems with horizontal dark bands. *E. hyemale* can
reach 4 ft. tall; *E. scirpoides* grows
only 6–8 in.

PLANTING: In moist soil or in water
to 6 in. deep for *E. hyemale* and to
1 in. deep for *E. scirpoides.* Invasive;
best in pots. Full sun or part shade.

PROPAGATION: Division

FILIPENDULA rubra
Queen of the prairie

HARDINESS: To −40°F/−40°C

SIZE: To 8 ft. tall, 4 ft. wide

DESCRIPTION: Plumes of pink
summer flowers above clump of
big, coarsely divided leaves.

Dormant in winter, even in mild
climates. 'Venusta', 4–6 ft. tall, has
purplish pink blooms.

PLANTING: In moist soil. Part or
full shade; can take full sun in cool-
summer climates.

PROPAGATION: Division

GLYCERIA maxima 'Variegata'
Variegated manna grass

HARDINESS: To −20°F/−29°C

SIZE: To 2–3 ft. tall, spreading by
rhizomes

DESCRIPTION: Straplike leaves
striped green, creamy yellow, and
white; often tinted pink in cool
weather. Smaller, more colorful,
a little less aggressive than basic
species; therefore a better choice.

PLANTING: In moist soil or in
water to 6 in. deep. Full sun or
part shade.

PROPAGATION: Division

Iris ensata

Hemerocallis 'Spider Man'

Hosta 'So Sweet'

Juncus effusus

HEMEROCALLIS hybrids
Daylily

HARDINESS: To −40°F/−40°C

SIZE: Variable: 1½ ft. tall and wide to 4 ft. tall, 3 ft. wide

DESCRIPTION: Evergreen, semi-evergreen, and deciduous types, all with arching, sword-shaped leaves and lilylike spring or summer flowers in yellow, orange, rusty red, pink, purple, apricot, buff, or cream, often with contrasting eyes or stripes. Some types rebloom later; others bloom throughout warm weather.

PLANTING: In moist, rich soil or in water to 4 in. deep. Full sun; need part shade in hottest climates.

PROPAGATION: Division

HOSTA spp.

HARDINESS: To −40°F/−40°C

SIZE: Variable: 1 ft. tall and wide to 3 ft. tall, 5 ft. wide (flower spikes often doubling height)

DESCRIPTION: Main feature is a broad mound of overlapping leaves, which are rounded to lance shaped, shiny or dull, smooth or textured, in green shades, chartreuse, blue, or gray. Many selections are edged or marked with a contrasting color. Thin spikes of lavender or white trumpet-shaped flowers in summer.

PLANTING: In moist, rich soil. Part or full shade.

PROPAGATION: Division

HOUTTUYNIA cordata 'Chameleon'

HARDINESS: To −20°F/−29°C

SIZE: To 9 in. tall, spreading by runners

DESCRIPTION: Red stems with heart-shaped green leaves splashed with cream, pink, yellow, and red; color most intense in sun. Small white summer flowers. Disappears in winter, even in mild climates.

PLANTING: In moist, rich soil or in water to 2 in. deep. Invasive; best in pots. Full sun or part shade.

PROPAGATION: Division

Houttuynia cordata 'Chameleon'

IRIS spp.

HARDINESS: Some species to −50°F/−46°C

SIZE: To 1½–5 ft. tall, spreading by rhizomes

DESCRIPTION: Swordlike green leaves and showy flowers. Water-loving species include blue flag, *I. versicolor* (violet-blue blooms); Japanese iris, *I. ensata* (purple, violet, pink, rose, red, white); *I. laevigata* (violet, magenta, white); and yellow flag, *I. pseudacorus* (bright yellow, ivory, pale yellow). Also Siberian irises (purple, blue, white, cream, yellow, pink, wine red) and Louisiana irises (wide range of colors), derived from several species.

PLANTING: In moist, rich soil or in water to 6 in. deep (to 10 in. deep for *I. pseudacorus*). Siberian irises won't tolerate standing water, and *I. ensata* tolerates it only during growing season. Full sun or light shade.

PROPAGATION: Division

Ligularia dentata
'Desdemona'

Liriope muscari

Lobelia
cardinalis

Ludwigia

Lysichiton americanus

JUNCUS spp.
Rush

HARDINESS: Some species to −30°F/−34°C

SIZE: To 2–5 ft. tall, 2–3 ft. wide

DESCRIPTION: Clump of leaflike, cylindrical green or gray stems and tiny flowers near stem tips. Most are grown for vertical form; corkscrew rush (*J. effusus* 'Spiralis') features twisting stems.

PLANTING: In moist soil or in water to 4 in. deep. Full sun or part shade.

PROPAGATION: Division

LIGULARIA spp.

HARDINESS: To −30°F/−34°C

SIZE: To 3–6 ft. tall, 3 ft. wide

DESCRIPTION: Stately clump of large rounded or lobed leaves topped by yellow to orange daisies in tall spikes on some species, branching clusters on others. Blooms in summer (into fall in some species).

PLANTING: In moist, rich soil. Most thrive in part or full shade.

PROPAGATION: Division

LIRIOPE spp.
Lilyturf

HARDINESS: Some species to 5°F/−15°C

SIZE: To 1–1½ ft. tall and wide

DESCRIPTION: Evergreen, glossy, dark green, grasslike leaves. Short white, lavender, or purple flower spikes in late summer and fall.

PLANTING: In moist, well-drained soil. Sun (except in hot, dry climates) to shade.

PROPAGATION: Division

LOBELIA cardinalis
Cardinal flower

HARDINESS: To −40°F/−40°C

SIZE: To 2–4 ft. tall, 1½–3 ft. wide

DESCRIPTION: Erect, single-stemmed plant with bronzy green leaves set directly on stem. Spikes of 1-in. scarlet tubular flowers in summer.

PLANTING: In moist soil. Tolerates water to 2 in. deep. Full sun or part shade.

PROPAGATION: Seed, division

LUDWIGIA spp.
Water primrose

HARDINESS: To 40°F/4°C

SIZE: Variable: from 2–3 in. to 6 ft. tall, some species spreading indefinitely

DESCRIPTION: Many species—some big and shrubby, others small and floating. Small, typically yellow flowers during warm weather.

PLANTING: In moist, rich soil or in water to 6 in. deep (1 in. for smaller types). Full sun or part shade.

PROPAGATION: Division, cuttings

LYSICHITON americanus
Yellow skunk cabbage

HARDINESS: To −30°F/−34°C

SIZE: To 4 ft. tall, 3 ft. wide

DESCRIPTION: Bright yellow spathes (hoods around flowers) to 1½ ft. long start appearing in early spring, before leaf-out. Paddle-shaped, shiny green leaves to 4 ft. long smell musky.

PLANTING: In moist soil or in water to 6 in. deep. Full sun or part shade.

PROPAGATION: Seed, division

Menyanthes trifoliata

Myriophyllum aquaticum

Mimulus cardinalis

Myosotis scorpioides

Nasturtium officinale

Mentha aquatica

MENTHA aquatica
Water mint

HARDINESS: To −10°F/−23°C

SIZE: To 6 in. tall in water or to 3 ft. tall on land, spreading by rhizomes

DESCRIPTION: Aromatic, 2½-in. bright green leaves on purplish stems. Round clusters of lilac flowers in summer.

PLANTING: In moist soil or in water to 5 in. deep. Invasive; best in pots. Full sun or part shade.

PROPAGATION: Division, cuttings

MENYANTHES trifoliata
Marsh trefoil, bog bean

HARDINESS: To −40°F/−40°C

SIZE: To 1 ft. high, 3 ft. wide

DESCRIPTION: Long-stalked, three-lobed, olive green leaves. Pink buds open to white or purplish star-shaped, fringed flowers in spring.

PLANTING: In moist soil or in water to 4 in. deep. Full sun or part shade.

PROPAGATION: Seed, division

MIMULUS spp.
Monkey flower

HARDINESS: Some species to −40°F/−40°C

SIZE: To 3 ft. tall and wide

DESCRIPTION: Water-loving species, all with snapdragonlike flowers on sprawling or upright stems, include *M. cardinalis* (red blooms), *M. guttatus* (yellow with red throat), and *M. ringens* (violet or white).

PLANTING: In moist soil. *M. ringens* can grow in water to 6 in. deep. Full sun or part shade.

PROPAGATION: Seed, division, cuttings

MYOSOTIS scorpioides
Water forget-me-not

HARDINESS: To −40°F/−40°C

SIZE: To 1 ft. tall and wide

DESCRIPTION: Sky blue, ¼-in. flowers with yellow eye from spring into fall. Shiny green, oblong leaves to 4 in. long. Self-sows.

PLANTING: In moist soil or in water to 3 in. deep. Full sun or part shade.

PROPAGATION: Seed, division

MYRIOPHYLLUM aquaticum
Parrot feather

HARDINESS: To −10°F/−23°C

SIZE: To 2½ ft. tall, spreading by rhizomes

DESCRIPTION: Whorls of feathery, emerald green leaves on trailing stems to 6 ft. long; tips emerge from water.

PLANTING: In water to 12 in. deep. Obtains nutrients from the water, so can be planted in gravel. Also grown as an oxygenator. Full sun or part shade.

PROPAGATION: Division

NASTURTIUM officinale
Watercress

HARDINESS: To −10°F/−23°C

SIZE: To 10−15 in. tall, 2−3 ft. wide

DESCRIPTION: Small, roundish, edible, dark green leaves with sharp, spicy flavor. Tiny white flowers. Self-sows.

PLANTING: In moist soil or in slow-running water to 3 in. deep. Full sun or part shade.

PROPAGATION: Seed, cuttings

Orontium aquaticum

Peltandra virginica

Nelumbo

Oenanthe javanica 'Flamingo'

Osmunda cinnamomea

NELUMBO spp.
Lotus

HARDINESS: To −30°F/−34°C, but best in warm climates

SIZE: To 2–6 ft. tall, spreading by rhizomes

DESCRIPTION: Big, round, green leaves to 2 ft. across. Fragrant white, cream, pink, red, or yellow flowers to 1 ft. wide stand above foliage in summer. Ornamental woody fruit, perforated like a saltshaker, follows.

PLANTING: In water to 24 in. deep for larger varieties, to 9 in. deep for smaller ones. Rhizomes are brittle, easily damaged. Full sun.

PROPAGATION: Division

OENANTHE javanica 'Flamingo'
Japanese watercress, water celery

HARDINESS: To 15°F/−9°C

SIZE: To 6 in. tall, spreading by rooting stems

DESCRIPTION: Celerylike edible leaves in bluish green edged with white and pink. Tiny white summer flowers.

PLANTING: In moist, rich soil or in water to 4 in. deep. Full sun or part shade.

PROPAGATION: Division, cuttings

ORONTIUM aquaticum
Golden club

HARDINESS: To −20°F/−29°C

SIZE: To 1–2 ft. tall, spreading by rhizomes

DESCRIPTION: Spear-shaped, waxy, bluish green leaves to 1 ft. long rise up in shallow waters, float in deeper waters. Spring flowers are whitish stalks with yellow tips.

PLANTING: In moist soil or in water to 18 in. deep. Full sun.

PROPAGATION: Seed, division

Osmunda regalis

OSMUNDA spp.

HARDINESS: To −40°F/−40°C

SIZE: To 2–6 ft. tall and wide

DESCRIPTION: Big deciduous ferns; green fronds turn orange, brown, and yellow in fall. Royal fern, *O. regalis,* and the smaller cinnamon fern, *O. cinnamomea,* are commonly grown.

PLANTING: In moist, rich soil. *O. regalis* can grow in water to 4 in. deep. Part or full shade; can take full sun in cool-summer areas.

PROPAGATION: Division

PELTANDRA virginica
Arrow arum

HARDINESS: To −20°F/−29°C

SIZE: To 3 ft. tall, 2 ft. wide

DESCRIPTION: Clump of glossy green, long-stemmed, foot-long leaves shaped like arrowheads. Greenish white summer flowers.

PLANTING: In moist soil or in water to 6 in. deep. May become invasive. Full sun or part shade.

PROPAGATION: Division

Phalaris arundinacea 'Picta'

Pontederia cordata

Primula

Rhynchospora colorata

Sagittaria latifolia

Saururus cernuus

PHALARIS arundinacea
Ribbon grass, lady's garters

HARDINESS: To −30°F/−34°C

SIZE: To 2–3 ft. tall, spreading by rhizomes

DESCRIPTION: Forms with colorful stripes on green, ribbonlike leaves include 'Feesey' ('Strawberries and Cream'), whose white stripes have some pink tinting; 'Tricolor', with white stripes and longer-lasting pink; 'Picta', with white stripes; and 'Luteopicta', with creamy yellow stripes.

PLANTING: In moist soil (tolerates drier soil) or in water to 2 in. deep. Invasive; best in pots. Full sun or part shade.

PROPAGATION: Division

PONTEDERIA cordata
Pickerel weed, pickerel rush

HARDINESS: To −40°F/−40°C

SIZE: To 2–4 ft. tall, 2½ ft. wide

DESCRIPTION: Long-stalked, glossy green, heart-shaped leaves to 10 in. long stand well above water. Blue flower spikes from late spring to fall.

PLANTING: In water to 6 in. deep. Full sun or light shade.

PROPAGATION: Seed, division

PRIMULA spp.
Primrose

HARDINESS: Some species to −20°F/−29°C

SIZE: To 2–3 ft. tall, 2 ft. wide

DESCRIPTION: Green foliage rosettes topped by flowers in spring, early summer. Moisture lovers include species with tiered blossoms: *P. japonica* (purple with yellow eye, white, or pink), *P. prolifera* (fragrant yellow), and *P. pulverulenta* (red to red-purple). *P. florindae* has clusters of fragrant, nodding yellow blooms.

PLANTING: In moist, rich, acid soil. Part or full shade; can take full sun in cool-summer climates.

PROPAGATION: Division

RHYNCHOSPORA colorata (Dichromena colorata)
Star sedge

HARDINESS: To 28°F/−2°C

SIZE: To 2 ft. tall, spreading by rhizomes

DESCRIPTION: Narrow, evergreen, grassy foliage. Star-shaped white flower bracts at stem ends in summer, sometimes into winter in mild climates.

PLANTING: In moist soil or in water to 2 in. deep. Full sun or light shade.

PROPAGATION: Seed, division

SAGITTARIA spp.
Arrowhead

HARDINESS: To −20°F/−29°C

SIZE: To 3 ft. tall and wide

DESCRIPTION: Big green leaves shaped like arrowheads. White, saucerlike summer flowers. *S. latifolia* has broad leaves. *S. sagittifolia* 'Flore Pleno' *(S. japonica)* has narrow leaves, double flowers.

PLANTING: In moist soil or in water to 6 in. deep. Full sun or part shade.

PROPAGATION: Division

SAURURUS cernuus
Lizard's tail, American swamp lily

HARDINESS: To −30°F/−34°C

SIZE: To 2–4 ft. tall, 5 ft. wide

Thalia dealbata

Schoenoplectus
tabernaemontani
'Albescens'

Spartina pectinata

Typha
angustifolia

Zantedeschia
aethiopica

DESCRIPTION: Heart-shaped, deep green leaves turn crimson in fall. Tiny, fragrant, creamy white summer flowers on thin, curving spikes.

PLANTING: In moist soil or in water to 6 in. deep. Full sun or part shade.

PROPAGATION: Division

SCHOENOPLECTUS tabernaemontani
Great bulrush

HARDINESS: To −30°F/−34°C

SIZE: To 4 ft. tall and wide

DESCRIPTION: Big clump of upright stems: dark green with horizontal yellow bands in 'Zebrinus'; nearly white with narrow, lengthwise green stripes in 'Albescens'.

PLANTING: In moist, rich soil or in water to 4 in. deep. Full sun or light shade.

PROPAGATION: Division

SPARTINA pectinata
Prairie cord grass

HARDINESS: To −30°F/−34°C

SIZE: To 7 ft. tall, spreading by rhizomes

DESCRIPTION: Long, ribbonlike foliage. Brown flower spikes in summer. 'Aureomarginata' has yellow leaf margins.

PLANTING: In moist or drier soil or in water to 6 in. deep. Full sun.

PROPAGATION: Division

THALIA dealbata
Water canna, hardy canna

HARDINESS: To −10°F/−23°C

SIZE: To 6–10 ft. tall, 6 ft. wide

DESCRIPTION: Long-stalked, paddle-shaped, bluish green leaves to 1½ ft. long. Foliage topped by violet-blue flower spikes to 8 in. long in summer.

PLANTING: In moist soil or in water to 24 in. deep. Full sun.

PROPAGATION: Division

TYPHA spp.
Cattail

HARDINESS: Some species to −40°F/−40°C

SIZE: To 1–10 ft. tall, spreading by rhizomes

DESCRIPTION: Long, swordlike or linear leaves. Cylindrical brown flowerheads in summer. Dwarf cattail *(T. minima),* 1–1½ ft. tall, best for small ponds. Other species need more space.

PLANTING: In moist soil or in water to 6 in. deep for *T. minima,* to 12 in. deep for larger species. Invasive; best in pots. Full sun or part shade.

PROPAGATION: Division

ZANTEDESCHIA aethiopica
Calla lily

HARDINESS: To 10°F/−12°C

SIZE: To 2–4 ft. tall, 2 ft. wide

DESCRIPTION: Evergreen to semievergreen, shiny green, arrow-shaped leaves. Pure or creamy white spathes to 8 in. long in spring, sometimes into summer. 'Green Goddess' has green-tipped spathes.

PLANTING: In moist, rich soil or in water to 12 in. deep. Full sun or light shade.

PROPAGATION: Division

CHAPTER SIX

Fish and Other Wildlife

FOR MANY, THE MAIN REASON *to have a water garden is to stock it with colorful fish. Constantly on the move and endlessly entertaining, ornamental fish like koi and goldfish include many varieties with features ranging from dramatic, multicolored patterns to flowing, deeply forked tails. Just watching these beautiful creatures can lift your spirits or soothe jangled nerves.* ❧ *Ornamental fish earn their keep in other ways, too. Garden pools are often plagued by excess algae, which turn the water green and line the sides of the pool. Fish help control some of that growth by feeding on it. They also devour mosquito larvae and other insects.* ❧ *In this chapter, you'll meet the most common kinds of fish suitable for ponds and other water gardens. You'll also learn how to care for fish through the seasons by providing an environment in which they can thrive. You'll even pick up tips on keeping predators at bay while welcoming desirable wildlife such as amphibians and turtles.*

Types of Fish

The traditional choices for ponds are koi and goldfish, because of their bright colors and easygoing habits. Other options include the diminutive mosquito fish for tub gardens and the colorful rainbow darter for enclosed streams. Descriptions of some fish well suited to water gardens appear on pages 160–163.

KOI

These ornamental fish are selectively bred strains of the common carp *(Cyprinus carpio).* Although color variations in carp had long been recorded, only several centuries ago did the Japanese begin breeding them for more distinctive and colorful markings. (The word "koi" comes from the Japanese *nishikigoi.)* Most varieties recognized by koi associations today have been around since the initial decades of the 20th century; the most recently developed breed dates from the 1950s.

VARIETIES Koi are classified by color, pattern, and scale type into more than a dozen major varieties, each in turn containing different types.

Most koi are solid colored or have two or three body hues. The color range includes red, orange, white, black, yellow, brown, and blue. On the multi-colored types, the hues are arranged in certain categorized patterns, though no two fish look exactly alike. Scale type further differentiates koi. The scales may be normal (like those of other fish); or they may cover only part of the fish; or they may be nonexistent. In some varieties, the scales have a diamondlike or pearly sheen.

The names given to different types of koi are Japanese descriptive words: for example, Bekko (black markings on a white, red, or yellow fish), Matsuba (dark-outlined scales), and Tancho (a red mark on the fish's head said to resemble the marking on a tancho crane). Background color designations include Shiro (white), Ki (yellow), and Aka or Hi (red). These terms may be combined, as in Shiro Bekko.

The most prevalent variety (and the first one developed) is Kohaku, featuring a distinctive red pattern on a white background. It was followed by Sanke, which incorporates a bit of black into the pattern. Next came Showa, in which the black predominates. These and other varieties are shown on pages 160–161.

PORTRAIT OF A KOI Under ideal conditions, koi will grow to 6 inches in the first year and reach about a foot in the second. They then put on 2 inches annually until they're nearly 2 feet long; thereafter, they continue to grow an inch or less per year. Genetics is a key determinant of ultimate koi size, though pond size, water quality, and food also affect growth rate. It's possible for a healthy specimen in a large pond

Big, energetic fish like koi need plenty of room, which an expansive pond like this provides. Clear water is essential for viewing the distinctive patterns and bright colors of koi.

to become 3 feet long and weigh more than 45 pounds.

Koi may live for 50 or 60 years, and sometimes even longer (the oldest known koi lived to be 226). This makes them lifetime companions, which suits their gregarious nature. Some will allow themselves to be petted, swim up when called, and follow their owners around the pond. They also get along well with other koi—though, while they don't normally eat other fish, they will eat their own eggs and newly hatched fry (young fish).

HOME, SWEET HOME Where winters are cold or summers sizzling, koi experts generally recommend a pool depth of 3 to 4 feet. In milder climates, koi can thrive in waters as shallow as 2 feet. Koi ponds often have biological filters, given the amount of waste the fish produce and the fact that they need good water quality year-round.

Many koi owners keep their ponds largely unplanted, because the fish often uproot plants with their snouts and even shred them. Others plant more sparsely than in a pond where plants are the main attraction; they choose tough species and secure the root systems in baskets.

When deciding on the type of home you want to provide for your koi, you may want to consult a local koi club. Members are usually happy to share their opinions and expertise.

A FISH PROFILE

A fish's sensory organs—eyes, nostrils, mouth, lateral line, and possibly barbels—allow the fish to locate food and discern dangers in its environment. The various fins work together to move the fish through the water and allow it to stop and to hover.

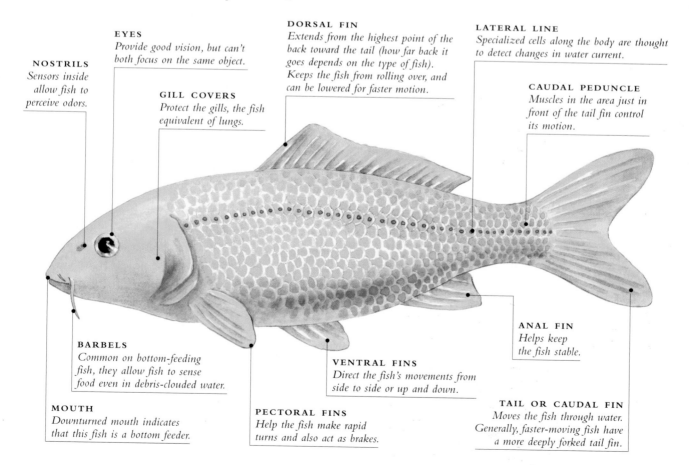

NOSTRILS
Sensors inside allow fish to perceive odors.

EYES
Provide good vision, but can't both focus on the same object.

GILL COVERS
Protect the gills, the fish equivalent of lungs.

DORSAL FIN
Extends from the highest point of the back toward the tail (how far back it goes depends on the type of fish). Keeps the fish from rolling over, and can be lowered for faster motion.

LATERAL LINE
Specialized cells along the body are thought to detect changes in water current.

CAUDAL PEDUNCLE
Muscles in the area just in front of the tail fin control its motion.

BARBELS
Common on bottom-feeding fish, they allow fish to sense food even in debris-clouded water.

MOUTH
Downturned mouth indicates that this fish is a bottom feeder.

VENTRAL FINS
Direct the fish's movements from side to side or up and down.

PECTORAL FINS
Help the fish make rapid turns and also act as brakes.

ANAL FIN
Helps keep the fish stable.

TAIL OR CAUDAL FIN
Moves the fish through water. Generally, faster-moving fish have a more deeply forked tail fin.

LEFT: *Goldfish will share waters companionably with koi as long as the koi are in the majority. The two kinds of fish shown here are similar in size, but the koi will soon grow larger than the goldfish.*

BELOW: *The easy-to-keep Common goldfish tolerates cold temperatures and poor water. The yellowish orange hue of this specimen looks like burnished metal.*

GOLDFISH

Distant cousins of koi, goldfish *(Carassius auratus)* are varieties of the Asian carp that have been bred for centuries as hobby fish. They contribute many hues— pure orange, bright red, pale yellow, black, and multicolors— to a pond. Some types of goldfish have a metallic sheen.

VARIETIES The Common (the original goldfish), Comet (larger fins and longer tail), and Shubun-kin (multicolored) all flourish year-round in outdoor ponds. Less cold-hardy types, like the Fantail and Veiltail (both with elaborate fins) and the Moor (vel-vety black), should be brought indoors where winters are cold. The Fantail, Veiltail, and Moor are all available in forms with telescope, or protruding, eyes.

Very exotic types include the Bubble-eye, which has delicate enlarged sacs around its eyes; the Celestial, with a perpetual upward gaze; and the Lionhead, with its raspberrylike head and absent dorsal fin. These are not well suited to outdoor ponds because they need a stable water temper-ature, free from fluctuations.

The fancier varieties are also typically smaller and slower than the more streamlined types, thus making it difficult for them to compete for food and exposing them to possible injury during the spawning season. Also, many have delicate fins that often become ragged in a pond.

ADAPTABILITY Goldfish are valued for their ability to tolerate varied conditions. Compared with koi, the size that goldfish can attain depends to a greater extent on the size of their home. Under ideal conditions, some varieties reach lengths of 16 inches; smaller varieties may attain 8. But because goldfish are smaller than koi, they can survive in ponds containing less oxygen, such as shallower ones (18 to 24 inches deep) or those with a lot of algae.

The typical life span of a goldfish in an outdoor pond is 6 to 12 years, but some have been known to defy the odds

rial breeder like a sunfish added to the pond may eat their eggs and fry, though there's no guarantee. In a naturalistic pond, consider more subtly colored species such as a school of killifish or a few sticklebacks.

Larger fish such as trout and catfish aren't suited to life in most garden ponds. But if you have a very large and fairly deep pond that you want to stock with game fish, check first with your state Department of Fish and Game. Raising certain species domestically is banned in some areas.

ABOVE: *A few mosquito fish in a tub garden like this will consume any mosquito larvae in the water. The rubber duckies are just for show— they don't control any insects.*

TOP LEFT: *In nature, rainbow darters are found in fast-moving streams. They also appreciate churned, well-aerated water, such as that found beneath waterfalls.*

and survive as long as 25 years if they receive good care.

Although goldfish are often territorial and aggressive, they will "school" with koi as long as the koi outnumber them. If your pond contains goldfish and no koi, filtration may not be necessary if you let the fish find their own food rather than feeding them. Goldfish produce less waste than koi and are more compatible with aquatic plants— they nibble on vegetation instead of ripping it apart. And intact plants help clean the pond, reducing the need for filtration (see "The Nitrogen Cycle" on page 164).

OTHER FISH

Diminutive fish are fine for tubs and other small water gardens. Although dull in color, mosquito fish are noticeable in a tub garden, where just a few will keep the tub free of insects. Some small fish, however, aren't suited to still water—the rainbow darter, for instance, is most at home in a fast-flowing stream or in small waterfalls or rapids feeding into a pond.

The fast-swimming golden orfe is a good candidate for an ornamental pond; it can share the waters with koi and goldfish. If you don't want your koi or goldfish to reproduce, a territo-

Fish for Water Gardens

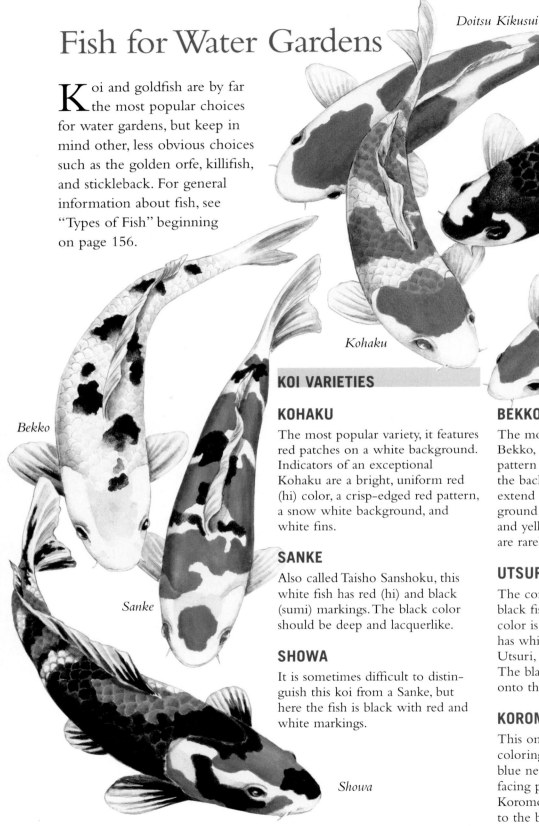

Koi and goldfish are by far the most popular choices for water gardens, but keep in mind other, less obvious choices such as the golden orfe, killifish, and stickleback. For general information about fish, see "Types of Fish" beginning on page 156.

Doitsu Kikusui

Utsuri

Kohaku

Bekko

Koromo

Sanke

Showa

KOI VARIETIES

KOHAKU

The most popular variety, it features red patches on a white background. Indicators of an exceptional Kohaku are a bright, uniform red (hi) color, a crisp-edged red pattern, a snow white background, and white fins.

SANKE

Also called Taisho Sanshoku, this white fish has red (hi) and black (sumi) markings. The black color should be deep and lacquerlike.

SHOWA

It is sometimes difficult to distinguish this koi from a Sanke, but here the fish is black with red and white markings.

BEKKO

The most common type is a Shiro Bekko, a white fish with a black pattern like stepping-stones down the back; the black usually does not extend to the head. Other background colors are red (Aka Bekko) and yellow (Ki Bekko), but these are rarely encountered today.

UTSURI

The complete variety name for this black fish with markings of another color is Utsurimono. Shiro Utsuri has white as a contrasting color; Hi Utsuri, red; and Ki Utsuri, yellow. The black color usually extends onto the head.

KOROMO

This one has the red-on-white coloring of a Kohaku, but with the blue netlike scales of an Asagi (see facing page) on the red patches. Koromo means "robed," a reference to the brocadelike pattern.

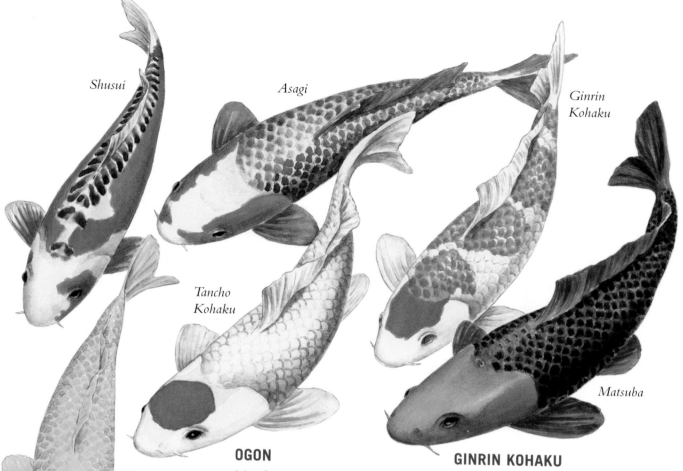

Shusui

Asagi

Ginrin Kohaku

Tancho Kohaku

Ogon

Matsuba

ASAGI

Its blue coloration is one of the natural carp colors. The entire back is covered in a netlike pattern of light blue or navy scales. There is red or orange on the flanks, fins, and tail. An unmarked, almost white head is the sign of a good specimen.

SHUSUI

An Asagi with the scales of a Doitsu, this is a pale blue fish with dark blue metallic scales along the back and red on the sides and fins.

OGON

Members of the Hikari group and the most recent variety of koi, Ogons have a metallic sheen throughout. Yamabuki Ogon is light yellow; Purachina Ogon, platinum; and Orenji Ogon, orange. Ogons with a single color are Hikarimono, and those with two or more are Hikarimoyo-mono. New color types are still being developed.

KOI TYPES WITHIN VARIETIES

TANCHO KOHAKU

This is a Kohaku whose only red is a spot on its head. Ideally, the red should be intense, be contained in as neat a circle as possible, and not extend to the eyes. The term "Tancho" may also be applied to other varieties, such as Tancho Sanke or Tancho Showa, provided that their only red is a spot on the head.

GINRIN KOHAKU

Koi with glittering scales are called Kinginrin, Ginrin, or just Gin. Shiny scales have been bred into almost all koi varieties; some look like diamonds or strings of pearls. Shown here, the typical red-and-white pattern of the Kohaku is covered in highly reflective scales.

DOITSU

Almost every koi variety is available as a Doitsu, which means "German scale"—the type was developed by crossing Japanese and German carp. The fish may have no scales at all ("leather carp") or a row of scales along the dorsal line. Kikusui (shown here) is a metallic Doitsu with a Kohaku pattern.

MATSUBA

Koi of any color can be Matsubas if their scales have black along with the underlying color. The look resembles a coat of mail.

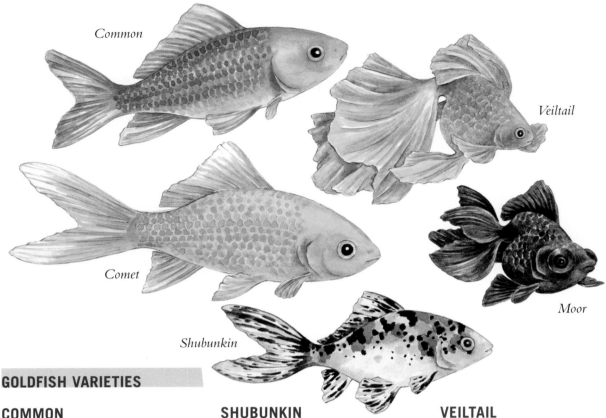

Common

Veiltail

Comet

Moor

Shubunkin

GOLDFISH VARIETIES

COMMON

This short-finned Chinese native is the original from which the fancy varieties were developed. An excellent swimmer and very hardy, it tolerates poorer water than do many other fish. Usually Commons are a bright, shiny, red-orange, but some types are yellow or silver. They grow from 8 to 16 inches long.

COMET

This U.S. native has a longer body, larger fins, and a more deeply forked tail fin than the Common. Fastest of the fancy goldfish, Comets are seen in yellow, orange, red, silver, and white forms. Sarassa is white with red markings; white with a red "cap" is Tancho. Comets grow from 8 to 16 inches long.

SHUBUNKIN

There are three shapes, all called Calico because of their coloring: pale blue flecked with red, orange, blue, black, and white. The Japanese Shubunkin shape is similar to that of a Comet; some have long, flowing tails. The London Shubunkin is shaped like the Common, and the Bristol Shubunkin is more rounded, with a big tail. All are fast swimmers and grow from 6 to 8 inches long.

FANTAIL

A Chinese variety, the Fantail has an oval body with a double tail and fins much longer than a Common's. This graceful, slow-swimming type includes the Calico (scaleless, with Shubunkin-like colors) and the Japanese (golden orange); it may have normal or telescope eyes. It grows from 6 to 8 inches long and must be brought indoors in cold weather.

VEILTAIL

This U.S. native with a round body and long, flowing tail and fins has a range of colors, but the most popular type is the multicolored Calico. The Telescope Veiltail has protruding eyes. All types grow from 6 to 8 inches long and must have indoor protection in cold weather.

MOOR

From China comes the only truly black goldfish. Its small, chunky body gets only 4 to 8 inches long. The original Moor is a black version of a telescope-eyed goldfish, with a shape like that of the Fantail. The Veiltail Moor is a black form of the Veiltail. Both need to be kept indoors in cold weather.

Fantail

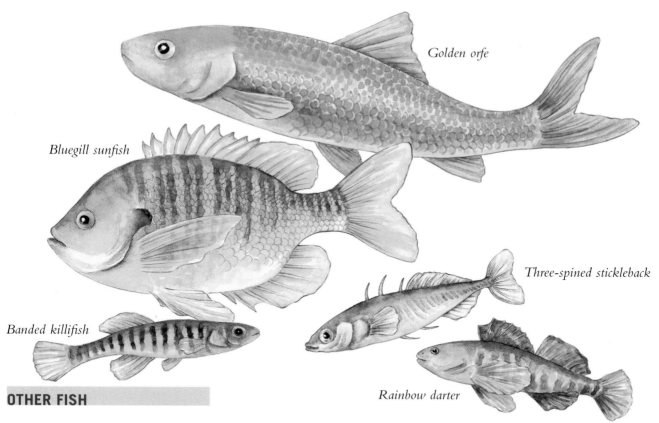

Golden orfe

Bluegill sunfish

Three-spined stickleback

Banded killifish

Rainbow darter

OTHER FISH

BANDED KILLIFISH
(Fundulus diaphanus)

Native from South Carolina to Newfoundland and inland along the St. Lawrence, the Great Lakes, and the upper Mississippi, this fish grows to about 3 inches long and lives about 3 years. It grazes at all pond levels. As a schooling fish, it's best in a group of about 12.

BLUEGILL SUNFISH
(Lepomis macrochirus)

These U.S. natives from east of the Rockies grow to about 10 inches long and live about 10 years. The male builds the nest and guards the eggs; introduce one male for every two or three females. Like other territorial breeders, sunfish may eat the eggs and fry of other fish. They also eat insects, mollusks, and crustaceans.

Mosquito fish

GOLDEN ORFE
(Leuciscus idus)

This fast-swimming European native needs a large pond, where it can reach 2 feet long and live about 15 years. It prefers well-aerated, deep water and eats zooplankton and fish (or it can be fed the same diet as koi). This schooling fish is best in groups of four or five. A sensitive species, it will not survive if exposed to chemicals in water.

MOSQUITO FISH
(Gambusia affinis)

Native from the Rio Grande to the Atlantic Ocean and from Florida to Delaware, it grows to 2 inches long and lives 1 to 3 years. The females (with dark spots on their sides) bear live young; the diet is insects, small fish, and crustaceans. Stock these schooling fish in groups of 5 to 50, depending on the pond size. They are often available for free from local mosquito control districts.

RAINBOW DARTER
(Etheostoma caeruleum)

Native to fast-flowing streams from New York State west to Minnesota and south to Mississippi and Alabama, it does best in streams or ponds with small waterfalls or rapids. It grows to 2½ inches long and lives 2 to 3 years, feeding on small insects and plankton.

THREE-SPINED STICKLEBACK
(Gasterosteus aculeatus)

This fish is native from Hudson Bay to the Atlantic coast and from Baffin Island to southern Virginia; on the West Coast, it's found from Baja California to southern Alaska. It grows to 3 inches long and lives about 4 years. The male (which becomes blue with a red belly during spawning season) builds the nest and guards the eggs. Sticklebacks are territorial and, for this reason, are best limited to two couples per pond. They eat insects, small fish, and crustaceans.

Fish Care

The requirements of fish-keeping are pretty much the same no matter which types of fish you choose for your water garden. Learn how to tend your charges, from preparing their water to feeding them and remedying any diseases.

BALANCING THE WATER

More than anything else, fish need good water quality. But don't confuse quality with clarity—the water may be clear yet still inhospitable to fish. It should contain plenty of oxygen (fish gasping at the surface at daybreak is a definite sign that it doesn't) but no harmful chemicals or excess algae. The pH level must be suitable for the type of fish—between 7.2 and 8.5 for koi and goldfish. To find out how to test and correct your water, see "The Importance of pH Levels" on page 179.

OXYGEN Fish absorb oxygen from water passing through their gills. Too little oxygen stresses fish, and a severe shortage can kill them. Ample oxygen is also essential to the survival of bacteria that break down wastes (see "The Nitrogen Cycle" below).

The greater the pond's surface area, the more oxygen it contains. But the supply diminishes as the water gets warmer in summer, exactly when fish are most active and need the most oxygen. To conserve oxygen, avoid crowding

The Nitrogen Cycle

In this natural process, beneficial bacteria convert ammonia produced by fish waste, pollen, and other organic debris into a form that plants can absorb or that escapes into the air. If enough bacteria are present, the nitrogen compounds (ammonia, nitrite, and nitrate) are eliminated and the water is clear and healthy for fish. The process slows down as the water temperature drops and the bacteria become less active.

The cycle can work naturally in a pond that contains only a few fish that are not fed plus a lot of plants. The more fish and fewer plants in the pond, the more likely it is that you'll have to give nature a hand with a biological filter containing the necessary bacteria (see page 58).

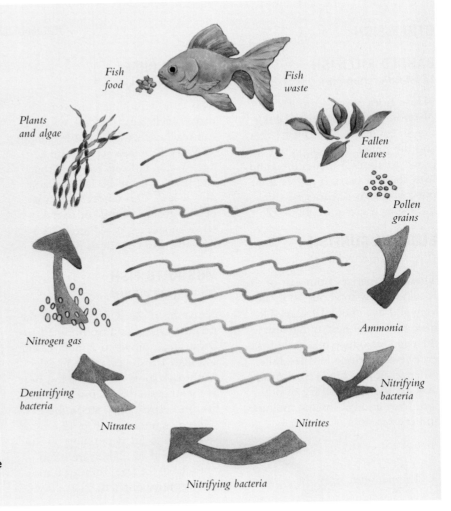

Fish food

Fish waste

Plants and algae

Fallen leaves

Pollen grains

Ammonia

Nitrifying bacteria

Nitrites

Nitrifying bacteria

Nitrates

Denitrifying bacteria

Nitrogen gas

the pond with too many fish. It's also important to keep the pond clean and not overfeed your fish. A fountain or underwater bubbler is a good source of extra aeration.

An excess of oxygenating, or submerged, plants can actually deprive fish of oxygen. Although plants produce oxygen as a by-product of photosynthesis, they do so only in daylight; at night, they consume it. Also, floating plants over too much of the pond surface can interfere with the exchange of gases between air and water. You may have to remove some plants—or fish—to reach the right balance.

HARMFUL CHEMICALS Ammonia is produced by fish waste and any other rotting debris such as uneaten fish food, leaves, and pollen grains. Too much ammonia encourages algae, which feed on it, to take over. When that happens, fish begin to die. In a pond containing a good balance of plants and fish, the beneficial bacteria can convert ammonia into a harmless substance.

Most municipal water supplies contain chlorine or chloramine (a combination of chlorine and ammonia). In large amounts these chemicals are deadly to fish, and even a small amount can kill the beneficial bacteria. Chlorine dissipates in a few days if the water is left standing, though a detoxifier (available at water garden suppliers and

This fountain located in a small pond set amid greenery isn't simply pretty to look at—it also aerates the pond water, ensuring that the fish get enough oxygen.

many pet stores) will eliminate it quickly. Chloramine must be treated by purifying the water at the source or adding a detoxifier to the pond. Ask your supplier what's in your water so you'll know how to proceed.

ALGAE Most new ponds go through a cloudy green stage, called "algae bloom," for 2 to 3 weeks after they're installed. Once aquatic plants or beneficial bacteria are established, they'll compete with those algae for nutrients, so the algae die off and the water clarifies. Algicides are also sold to kill algae, but they don't control ammonia, so they must be used in ponds with biological filters or you put your fish at risk. Too much algicide also damages water plants.

That same explosion of green water is to be expected every year in early spring when the water warms up. The pond should regain its balance as plants put on spring growth and the

beneficial bacteria resume their role in the nitrogen cycle.

WATER CHANGES. If you have a biological filter (see page 58), there's seldom a reason to change the water. But if you must flush out any accumulating nitrates, siphon or pump out some water and put more in, rather than just topping off the pond. Never change more than 20 percent of the pond volume at once, unless you're removing the fish and cleaning the pond.

When topping off a pond, add water where it's not directly touching the fish—for example, at a waterfall or through a spray nozzle (a fine spray also aerates the pond). If your water contains chlorine, never lay the hose in the water; fish attracted to the flow may suffer gill burn. Before adding water that contains either chlorine or chloramine, protect the fish and the beneficial bacteria by treating your pond with a detoxifier.

BUYING FISH

To find a reputable dealer, ask a friend or neighbor with a fish pond for a referral; for koi, inquire at a local koi club. Also check the resources on page 188. Don't bring the fish home until the pond is ready for them: If the pond is newly planted, wait at least a month for the plantings to establish themselves. If it's unplanted, just test the water to make sure it's free of any harmful chemicals.

Start with small to medium-size fish; very young ones may not make the adjustment to your pond, and fully grown fish are usually quite expensive. Your new pond inhabitants will probably adapt better if you select a few rather than a single specimen. If you're buying koi for the first time, look for ones 4 to 8 inches long; goldfish should be 2 to 4 inches long. Be aware that young goldfish won't yet have their distinctive colorings, nor young koi their final color patterns.

Observe the fish before you choose. Healthy fish are active. They should not be hanging listlessly in midwater or hovering at the bottom of the tank. Their fins should be intact and held erect, and they should not be rubbing against the tank. Their skin should be free of sores and their eyes bright.

For transport, have the dealer place the fish in a plastic bag containing a small amount of water and a blast of pure oxygen. Put the bag in a box and cover it to protect the fish from the sun. Also guard it from heat (for instance, don't transport the box in a car trunk).

How Many Fish?

Experts recommend stocking a pond lightly at first, then gradually adding more fish as you get a better feel for the pond's capacity. A good rule of thumb is one koi (assuming it will grow to 18 inches long) for every 100 gallons of water and 4 inches of fish length of other kinds for every 30 gallons.

Sizable koi can be expensive. When you buy them young and small, don't expect them to look like this— their characteristic patterns and colors will develop as they grow.

INTRODUCING FISH

Late spring or early summer is a good time to introduce fish to the water garden, but they can be released in winter in mild climates.

Don't just spill a fish out of the plastic bag it came in. Float the bag on the surface for 15 to 20 minutes (45 to 60 minutes in winter), so that the water temperature in the bag can gradually approximate that of the pond. Shade the bag with a wet towel on a warm, sunny day. If the fish is going from hard water to softer water or vice versa, you can open the bag and add a cup of pond water every 5 or 10 minutes to let it adjust to the new pH level.

Then, gently turn the open bag upside down so the fish can swim out. It may hide for a few days, but soon it will come out and begin to feed.

ABOVE: *Release newly acquired fish only after acclimating them to your pond water. On a sufficiently warm or sunny day, you should shade the bags to protect the fish.*

BELOW: *The number of fish your pond can support depends on its size. Quite a few will fit in a pond this big, but it's best to start out conservatively and add to your stock over time.*

Scatter floating food pellets on the water to bring bottom feeders like koi to the surface. These koi have roiled the water in their eagerness to feed.

FEEDING

Fish don't really need to be fed in a balanced pond containing insects, algae, and a lot of aquatic plants—all of which fish eat. But if your pond has few plants or if you enjoy the interaction with your fish, feed them—but give them only as much as they can consume in 5 minutes. (Neither koi nor goldfish have stomachs for storing food, so be careful not to overfeed them.)

Goldfish and koi are omnivorous; they eat almost anything. Packaged foods containing a balance of protein, carbohydrates, and vitamins meet their nutritional needs. Basic rations can be supplemented with worms, daphnia (water fleas), brine shrimp, and ant eggs; frozen or dried forms of these treats are less likely to carry disease. Koi also like fresh vegetables such as lettuce and peas.

SEASONAL FLUCTUATIONS Fish digest food more efficiently in warmer water, so feed them during the day rather than at night. As cold weather approaches, feed them progressively less until the water temperature dips below 50°F/10°C; then stop altogether. (A pond thermometer is a reliable way to tell how cold the pond is.) At 45°F/7°C, fish stop eating and hibernate at the bottom of the pond.

Many koi owners say that interacting with their fish at feeding time is among the most rewarding aspects of owning them. The koi will often accept food directly from their owner's hand.

Fish live off their body fat until warmer water in spring rouses them. Their digestion is still slow at winter's end, so feed them sparingly until the water warms to 65°F/19°C; after that, you may feed them routinely. Fish are stressed in very warm water, so also reduce feeding when the pond temperature exceeds 80°F/27°C.

VACATION FEEDING Even in a pond with few plants, fish can go without being fed for up to a couple of weeks. If you will be gone longer, use an autofeeder or measure out food for a friend or neighbor to dispense. Keep in mind that without exact allocations, most people tend to overfeed fish.

In early spring, as the water slowly warms up, koi are gradually coming out of hibernation and aren't yet ready for regular feedings.

Fine Food

- Floating pellet foods are best; they attract bottom feeders like koi and goldfish to the surface so you can enjoy watching them, and any uneaten food can be skimmed off with a net. Choose a pellet size appropriate for your smallest fish. If you wish, you can give larger pellets to the larger fish.
- For cold-weather feeding, choose a food rich in easily digested wheat germ.
- Products labeled as koi food often contain higher levels of protein (sometimes in the form of spirulina algae) than does standard food, which is a plus for large, active fish.
- Foods with color enhancers such as carotene and algae meal intensify existing colors (but don't create new colors) in goldfish and koi. Use enhancers in moderation; overuse distorts white to a pinkish color and causes reds and blacks to become brassy.

Keep an eye on your fish so you can take care of any problems right away. The deckside location of this pond makes it easy to observe the goldfish and to notice if they're swimming oddly or rubbing up against the rocks.

FISH DISEASES

Because stressed fish are more prone to disease, be sure to treat your fish well and keep their home in tip-top shape. Observe them regularly, with a eye to nipping problems in the bud.

PREVENTION Reduce the stress factors that you can control —first of all, provide fish with deep waters to protect them from predators (see page 173) and temperature swings. But whether your pond is deep or shallow, you can avoid other stresses such as overcrowding, rough handling, insufficient oxygen, and toxins in the water.

Maintain good water quality (see pages 164–165) and check your fish often for such symptoms as appetite loss, fins held abnormally close to the body, skin sores, rubbing on pond walls and other surfaces, and erratic swimming. If you need to remove a fish from the pond, scoop it out with some of the water in a bowl or bucket rather than risk damaging it in a net. If you must touch a fish, wet your hands first so you don't rub off the transparent slime coating that protects it from infection.

BREEDING

During breeding season, in spring and early summer, you may notice fish splashing around and males chasing after females. Rambunctious koi can actually push each other out of the pond; lower the water level to prevent this. Some types of pond fish give birth to live young, but more typically females deposit eggs on underwater plants and males fertilize the eggs.

You might not want the fish to increase, since that could upset the pond's balance. Nature may keep the numbers in check: many fish eat their own eggs and those of other species, and other pond creatures also feed on fish eggs. To promote population control, either keep the pond free of plants (and thus nesting sites) or try stocking a territorial breeder like a sunfish that may consume any fish eggs and fry.

If you want to breed your fish, you can temporarily move spawning fish to a holding tank or blocked-off area of the pond. Or put a spawning mop in the pond. After the fish spawn, move the mop to an area where the fry can develop in safety.

Be prepared to cull the fry, since breeding may produce deformed or otherwise undesirable fish. You'll soon learn that young koi and goldfish do not necessarily resemble their parents in color or pattern. Also note that, though koi and goldfish can interbreed, the result will always be a goldfish.

TREATMENT Salt relieves stress in fish, and it can clear up many diseases. Add 8 pounds of marine salt for every 1,000 gallons of water in your pond. The aquatic plants can easily tolerate this concentration. You can isolate a sick fish for a more concentrated salt bath—3 ounces of dissolved salt per gallon for about 10 minutes.

Water garden suppliers and pet stores sell many fish medications as well as medicated fish food. But without a reliable diagnosis from a veterinarian or experienced pondkeeper, dosing a sick fish is usually a hit-or-miss proposition. Look for assistance, and don't get into the habit of uncorking chemicals at the first sign of trouble. And if you have a biological filter, be sure that a particular product will not harm the bacteria in your filter media.

COMMON DISEASES

DISEASE	TYPE	SYMPTOMS	REMEDY
Anchor worm	Parasite	Threadlike worms, to ½ in. long, attach themselves to skin. Twin egg sacs may be visible at end.	Salt bath; antiparasitic treatment; removal with tweezers
Cloudy eye	Nonspecific	Milky cloud covers the eyes; the fish loses energy and appetite.	Improved water quality; salt bath; antibiotics
Dropsy (pinecone disease)	Nonspecific	Scales stand out from body like a pinecone opening; the eyes bulge. Swollen abdomen is common. Often fatal by the time the symptoms appear.	Same treatment as for cloudy eye
Finrot/tailrot	Bacteria	Begins with light, foggy patches; progresses to bloody and rotted fins or tail.	Same treatment as for cloudy eye
Fish lice	Parasite	Lice are clear and flat, to ¼ in. across, and hard to see without magnification. Fish rubs against pool sides in effort to "brush off" lice.	Salt bath; antiparasitic treatment
Flukes (gill or skin)	Parasite	Gill flukes: Fish swims with jerky motion, gasps at surface or faces the side of pond as if exhausted. Skin flukes: Skin appears whitish; fish rubs against objects in pool.	Salt bath; antiparasitic treatment
Fungus disease (cotton disease)	Fungus	Whitish or greenish strands that look like cotton or wool hang from fish. Fungus usually attacks previously injured fish.	Salt bath; antifungal treatment
Ich (white spot)	Parasite	White spots like salt appear on body and fins; on closer view, "noodlelike" parasites may be visible. Fish rubs against objects. Often fatal if spots cover fish.	Salt bath; antiparasitic treatment
Ulcer (hole-in-the-side disease)	Bacteria	Open sores appear on body. This is a contagious, often fatal, disease.	Improved water quality; antibiotics

Regularly skimming leaves and other debris from a pond will help keep the water in good condition. In cold-winter climates, it's especially important to groom the pond in autumn, before it ices over.

Safeguarding Fish in Winter

Fish sold for outdoor ponds in wintry climates should be able to safely spend the coldest months of the year outside. But the pond must be at least 3 to 4 feet deep, to protect the fish from prolonged cold and to keep the pond from freezing solid. (If you have a shallower pond or small tub garden, overwinter the fish indoors in an aquarium.)

GET READY

Remove fallen leaves and other debris from the water during autumn. Organic material that decomposes underwater emits methane gas, which can kill fish if it builds up to toxic levels.

Place netting over the pond to catch debris in winter. If practical, you may want to build a cover that also helps insulate the pond—for example, make a wooden frame layered with straw and wrapped in a tarp. Be sure it's sturdy enough to withstand strong winds and an accumulation of snow.

Once the water temperature sinks below 52°F/11°C, you may shut off the biological filter and any waterfall or fountain. In any case, you should definitely turn them off when the temperature drops below 39°F/4°C, to avoid mixing colder water near the surface with warmer water below.

OPEN OR CLOSED?

Some pond owners keep a part of the pond free of ice, but others don't bother—fish can survive winter nicely at the bottom of a pond that's frozen over.

If you want an opening, don't heat the whole pond. Use a small floating pool heater or de-icer to keep a hole open; it emits just enough heat to maintain the area around it ice-free. Run it only

If you decide to keep your pond open in winter, all you need to thaw is a small circle in the ice rather than a large area of the pond.

when the water temperature is near freezing, to avoid wasting electricity (some models are pre-set to turn on automatically).

Don't bang on the ice to open it—the vibrations can stress fish. Instead, melt the ice by setting a pan of boiling water on it. You can also siphon off a little pond water to create an insulating layer of warmer air beneath the ice.

SPRING TASKS

As temperatures begin to rise in spring, add extra bacteria to the biological filter and check your fish for any signs of damage or disease (see pages 170–171). To maintain the pond itself and its equipment, consult page 180.

Pond Protection

Because your fish live outdoors, various predators will consider them fair game. Raccoons and herons or other "fishing" birds are among the biggest threats to fish. You'll want to take precautions, especially if you live near open or wild land (though raccoons are common almost everywhere).

SMART DESIGN

The best defense against predators is to design your pond so as to frustrate them. Make the pond 2 feet or deeper throughout. Raccoons feel their way into water, so fairly steep sides keep them from finding solid footing to use as a ladder. Without a shallow area that allows easy swipes at fish, cats are usually content to sit pondside and just watch.

Many ponds contain a shelf around the inside perimeter for plants; fill it completely full so raccoons can't use it as a step. Dense plantings around the outside of the pond deter herons, which like to wade gradually down a muddy bank.

Provide your fish with hiding places, such as ledges under which they can swim or sections of terra-cotta pipe laid at the bottom of the pond. These hide-outs should be beyond the reach of predators or too small for the predators to enter.

In addition, don't leave pet food outdoors—it attracts wildlife.

OTHER PLOYS

If you've inherited a pond that isn't designed to thwart predators, you still have some other tricks to try. A good general deterrent is an alert dog in the yard.

A low-voltage electric fence around the garden keeps land-bound predators like raccoons away. If that isn't practical, you can place wire mesh around or over the pond—although it may detract from the pond's appearance.

Lightweight netting over the pond foils marauding birds, if they're your main problem, but it too may be unsightly. Some pond owners successfully impede kingfishers with trip lines (clear fishing line strung in a crisscross pattern over the water).

Noisemakers, scarecrows, decoys, and mock predators such as floating alligator heads are other ploys often recommended to deter predatory birds. They may work only temporarily, until the birds realize they don't pose a genuine threat. As for decoys, be forewarned that placing a heron statue in the pond may attract other herons. Finally, if you have dangerous visitors like alligators, call the state Department of Fish and Game for assistance.

Giving your fish hiding places such as sections of terra-cotta pipe laid on the bottom of the pond will help protect them from persistent predators like herons.

Desirable Wildlife

Your water garden can be a home for more than just fish. A wide range of wildlife either lives in water all the time or needs a pond for part of its life cycle. A pond or other water feature also draws birds.

THEY WILL COME

A well-designed pond that fits seamlessly into your landscape is a magnet for wild creatures; they show up on their own even when natural waterways are miles away. This is especially true when you create a hospitable environment with lots of plants. Some pond owners ensure wildlife by transferring a bucket of water and mud containing microscopic organisms from a local pond to their own. (Make sure there are no legal restrictions before doing this.)

But before you lay out the welcome mat, decide whether you really want a water garden teeming with diverse wildlife. If your main interest is ornamental fish, you probably want a fair number of them, which can make keeping other wildlife difficult. For example, a large population of fish can eat enough amphibian eggs and young to keep them from reproducing successfully. Also, turtles and amphibians need a pathway in and out of the pond. While providing sloped or shallow sides and basking islands is great for them, it also guarantees access for fish predators.

If you decide in favor of diverse wildlife, then you're probably better off with fewer fish. Or you can stock the pond with inexpensive minnows or feeder goldfish (the kind raised as food for larger fish or other aquatic life). Some of these may even survive and grow into decent-size fish.

AMPHIBIANS These creatures—frogs, toads, salamanders, and newts—eat insects in the water, and their spawn provides live food for fish. Some adult amphibians may also occasionally take a small fish or two. Although they can be introduced as eggs or tadpoles, amphibians don't seem to have trouble locating ponds on their own.

Many species of frogs and newts live in the pond for much of their life cycle. Some, such as the wood frog, normally live on land and use the pond only to spawn. Salamanders need an aquatic environment to spawn, but otherwise spend their life on land, buried underground. Toads, which also live on land and use the pond to breed, are especially welcome because they eat earwigs and other insect pests in the surrounding garden.

If you want frogs and toads, be prepared for a lot of croaking, usually at night. The many species vary in their vocalizations, which some people find soothing and others (usually the neighbors of water gardeners) find irritating.

Frogs and toads are frequent—and usually welcome—visitors to garden ponds. While some species live in ponds, others make their homes on land but spawn in the water.

LEFT: *Turtles sunning themselves on rocks can be mistaken for garden statuary. Be sure to alert visitors to their presence. It's easy to trip when the "statuary" begins to move unexpectedly.*

BELOW: *A birdbath of any type, as long as it contains even a little water, is a surefire way to attract birds to your yard.*

TURTLES Adult turtles of most species that might make your pond their home are omnivorous, eating plants, insects, algae, tadpoles, frogs, and small fish. Aquatic turtles tend to eat a lot, adding significantly to the waste that your pond filter has to handle. And even a well-fed turtle may attack fish, so mix the two only if the pond is big enough for the fish to avoid the turtles. As turtles like to bask in the sun, they'll appreciate large flat rocks near the water's edge or protruding from the pond.

Avoid snapping turtles, which can be dangerous. If you bring in turtles, choose species native to your area: if they wander off (which they may do if not fenced in), natives can probably find another suitable habitat. Also, locally adapted turtles can spend the winter hibernating at the bottom of your pond and don't have to be brought indoors.

BIRDS A pond will increase the number of birds that find their way to your garden. Encourage them to stay by furnishing nearby shelter and food in addition to the water your pond provides. Shelter can take the form of brambles or other twiggy cover, or you can install birdhouses. Keep birds well fed by surrounding the pond with plants that produce a lot of seeds, flowers, or berries.

The sound of moving water attracts birds, but most prefer water they can wade into. A pebble beach edging one side of the pond will ease their access, but may also encourage predators. You might provide other water sources nearby, such as birdbaths or even rocks with deep indentations that will hold water.

CHAPTER SEVEN

Water Garden Maintenance

ALL GARDENS REQUIRE MAINTENANCE, *and water gardens are no exception. But the work involved is not all that much, and it's really a small price to pay for the beauty and pleasure a water feature provides. Many companies provide pond services if you don't want to do the work yourself.*

Although a pond's structure presents few problems, everything within it will need periodic attention. The water must be clean and balanced, the pumps and filters must function smoothly, and accessory lighting will need adjustment. The good news is that most chores are parceled out by seasons, spreading the effort around the year. You'll find that a seasonal rhythm to the process develops naturally, as it does for other yard maintenance, so that caring for your water garden will become as routine as looking after a vegetable or flower garden. Basically, it's a matter of keeping the water clean and healthy and tending to any plant or animal life it contains.

Maintaining the Water

In a water feature without plants or fish, clean, clear water can be maintained with chemicals, as a swimming pool is. In a pond containing fish, clear water is mainly an aesthetic choice—the fish don't care, but it's nice to be able to see them easily. Maintaining water clarity is relatively straightforward; see the troubleshooting chart on the right that lists symptoms and solutions based on water color.

Beyond clarity is health: a pond with living organisms in it must be monitored to provide them with the appropriate algae populations and pH levels.

ALGAE: GOOD, BAD, AND UGLY

Algae are a form of plant life common to all ponds. There are literally hundreds of types, from floating, single-celled planktonic algae to stringy, filamentous ones. The chief problem in garden ponds is an excess of algae, and the key to controlling this is to control the nutrients the algae feed on.

Crystal clear water is not necessary for the health of your fish but it is certainly more aesthetically pleasing. Sparkling water also better reflects the surrounding plants and trees.

Algae growth depends on ammonia, a natural by-product of decomposing plant debris and fish waste. Ammonia is continually forming in water; it can kill fish even in very low concentrations, but in nature it's controlled by bacteria, which break it down, and by algae, which consume it. If sufficient bacteria are present (see "The Nitrogen Cycle" on page 164), the pond water will be clear and healthy for fish. If there are insufficient bacteria, and ammonia levels begin to increase, algae spores blowing around in the air will colonize the pond. The algae then grow

QUICK GUIDE TO TROUBLESHOOTING MURKY WATER

WATER COLOR	CAUSE	REMEDY
Pea soup green	Algae	Increase biological filtration; add UV light; use algicide or flocculants.
Yellow	Decaying leaves	Net out leaves at bottom of pond; skim surface leaves off daily; add leaf- or sludge-digesting bacteria.
Reddish brown	Silt buildup	Vacuum bottom; strip-clean pond (see page 183); add silt-digesting bacteria.
Red	High iron content	Increase aeration.
Milky white	Bacterial bloom	Be patient—problem will resolve itself in a new pond.
Black	Extensive pollution	Completely drain and strip-clean pond.

by consuming the ammonia, and the pond turns green. This is called an algae bloom. (See "Balancing the Water" on page 164.)

All ponds are susceptible to an algae bloom in the spring, as the pond revives. Algae blooms are also almost guaranteed in new ponds, before a balance can form in the fresh water. Elimination of all algae is not the goal; at the right levels, some algae types are beneficial to the pond environment. For example, the thin layer of algae that forms on the sides and bottoms of ponds works as a biofilter does and should not be scrubbed away.

UV LIGHTS FOR ALGAE CONTROL
An ultraviolet (UV) clarifier is another effective way to reduce the algae that turn pond water pea soup green. The device is simply a long ultra-violet light inside a PVC pipe, suspended in the pond (see photo on page 59). Water is pumped through the pipe and past the light, which sterilizes the algae. Although UV clarifiers can turn green water clear in a few days, they are fairly expensive and must be matched to the size of the pond to work effectively. When adding a UV clarifier, connect it in line after the biofilter, which is also controlling algae. And, as with any other artificial algae control, be sure to monitor the ammonia levels when the clarifier is first installed. Ammonia test kits are available in pond supply outlets.

THE IMPORTANCE OF pH LEVELS

Just as soil pH affects your garden plants' growth, water pH determines whether your pond's inhabitants will thrive. When pH (potential hydrogen) levels are too high, they are referred to as alkaline; low levels are acid. An extreme of either is harmful to both fish and plants. The ideal pH range of a stable pond with fish is between 7.2 and 8.5. (Uninhabited ponds have more leeway: from 6.5 to 9.5.) If your level is beyond these parameters, you'll need to take corrective steps—but not too quickly. A rapid change of pH can stress fish more than either extreme might. As a rule, the pH level should not alter by more than .2 points within a 2-hour period. New water features should be balanced before fish are added.

Many easy-to-use pH testers are on the market. If your reading reveals a problem, stabilizing additives to correct the imbalance are also available in pool and pet supply stores.

Although the heavy planting in this pond is attractive, too many floating leaves can interfere with the exchange of gases between air and water, making it difficult for fish to get enough oxygen.

Seasonal Care

Each season of the year brings changes to the pond, from fluctuating water temperatures to algae bloom to leaves falling on the surface. The key to keeping pond water clean and the fish and plant life healthy through all these changes is regular maintenance and attention to details.

SPRING

Plants bloom in the spring—and that includes algae. Their growth is directly related to increased sunshine and warming waters, which can combine to create an algae bloom. This is in part because algae grow faster than do the beneficial bacteria that help control them. The main reason that an algae bloom is almost guaranteed in a new pond is that algae-controlling bacteria have not yet had time to establish a full colony.

If you have a biological filter (see page 58) you'll need to replace last year's colony of beneficial bacteria, which may have died off over the winter. To do so, add a new colony as soon as your fish become active in the warming water. If you are otherwise properly caring for your pond, the water will soon clear.

Spring is also a time to clean up your water plants. Bring up plants anchored in submerged baskets. Wash the muck from the baskets and trim away the dead leaves or stalks. Similarly, clean up the dead leaves and branches from plants along the water's edge.

At the same time, dredge up dead leaves and other debris from the pond's bottom. Shut off the pump, rake out large leaves, and let the water settle for an hour. When much of the sediment has sunk to the bottom, direct a shop vacuum hose along the bottom to remove the muck. The fish will flee the disturbance.

Finally, pull out the pump and clean the filter. Check the electrical cord for any damage; replace it if needed. Wipe any muck or algae off the lights.

SUMMER

By summer, plant and fish life are in full growth, and possibly the algae as well. If the water is still pea green, your biofilter may be not working properly, or it may be of insufficient size. If adding new bacteria doesn't clear the water within a week or two, consider installing a larger biofilter. For ponds without biofilters, you can add more oxygenating and floating-leaf plants or reduce the number of fish your pond contains. If you still have excess algae, you may want to purchase

The greenish water in this pond is typical of a spring algae bloom and can normally be cleared up quickly by the addition of a new colony of bacteria to the biological filter.

an ultraviolet light water clarifier.

Marginal plants can now be divided into smaller clumps and replanted. Summer is also a good time to add new fish and plants to the pond.

To protect newly hatched fish, called fry, be sure there are numerous baskets of plants in the pond. The fry can hide from larger fish by tucking in among the leaves and stems.

Warm summer weather causes the pond water to evaporate more quickly. If you have a float valve hooked to a water source, turn it off for a week to see how much water the pond loses. Check the water level weekly and top it off, adding a chlorine/chloramine detoxifier if needed. When topping off, it's best to add the water by spraying it over the surface; this allows some of the chlorine to evaporate before it lands in the pond.

AUTUMN

Autumn means leaves falling on the pond. Skim the pond daily or stretch a net over the surface to hold the leaves until you can remove them.

Trim away dead leaves and branches on plants around the pond margin, but do not cut hollow-stalked plants below the water level; this may kill them.

Monitor fish carefully for signs of parasites or stress. (See "Common Diseases" on page 171.)

WINTER

As the temperature drops, fish go into a form of hibernation. When the water drops down to 50°F/10°C, they often hang almost motionless in the deepest part of the pond. Curiously, their colors are most intense at this time. When the water temperature is between 54 and 59°F/ 13 and 16°C, feed the fish only

As leaves turn in the fall they begin to drop into the pond. Be prepared to scoop them out regularly to avoid heavy algae growth due to the extra organic matter present.

once a day; between 50 and 54°F/10 and 13°C, feed them just once a week. Stop feeding entirely when temperatures stay below that.

You can turn off the pump when pond temperatures drop below 52°F/11°C; you must do so when they're below 39°F/ 4°C, which is the temperature winter ponds often reach at the pond's bottom. This water is dense and well oxygenated. Because the colder water rises to the top, you must avoid circulating the pond, which mixes the colder surface water with the warmer bottom water.

Cleaning Your Pond

Some people completely drain and clean their pond once a year. It is best to do this in the fall, because that's when the fish are putting on fat for the winter and are more resistant to stress, but anytime during the growing season will do. Other fish pond owners never perform this "strip clean." If you do strip-clean your pond, be careful not to overdo it. That thin layer of beneficial algae on the sides and bottom of the pool is vital to the pond's long-term health. When cleaning the pond, wash it down with a hose, but do not scrub away that layer. When the pool is refilled, those algae will quickly resume supporting the beneficial bacteria that help maintain proper water chemistry.

CLEANING TOOLS

Before you start cleaning, go over the tool and equipment list below to make sure you have the necessary materials. Having them on hand will make the project go that much faster and easier.

- Rubber gloves and boots
- Fishnet
- Holding tank for fish
- Shop vac or wet/dry vac
- Hose and spray nozzle
- Submersible pump

TRANSFERRING FISH

You must remove the fish and put them in holding tanks while the pond is being cleaned. It is important to do this carefully to minimize the stress on the fish.

For fish under 12 inches long, use one or more 30-gallon rubber garbage containers. The finish applied to new containers can be toxic to fish, so scrub them with salt and water until the plastic smell is gone. Fish over 12 inches long should be held in 50- to 100-gallon containers. Ideal for this purpose are the galvanized metal watering troughs for horses. Pump water from the pond into the trough, letting it splash and aerate.

Net fish less than 12 inches long and lower them gently into the holding tank. Fish longer than 12 inches should not be lifted into the air in a net. Instead, herd them to the end of the pool and net them one at a time. Then have a helper scoop each fish, with plenty of pond water, into a large plastic bag and transfer it gently to the holding tank.

No aeration is needed if the pond cleaning is completed within 4 or 5 hours, but the holding tank water must be kept close to its original temperature. Keep the tanks in the shade, even if it means building a temporary shade structure. The warmer the water gets, the less oxygen it holds, and the more stressed the fish become.

Larger fish must be moved individually to a holding tank in plastic bags. Koi are relatively docile; they will swim slowly and calmly as you gently herd them to one end of the pond and bag them from inside the net.

HOW TO STRIP-CLEAN A POND

Pump the water from the pond. Some biofilters can be switched to a drain mode to pump water out. If you're using a submersible pump, stop pumping just before the inlet is exposed to air. The nutrient-rich pond water can be pumped directly onto your lawn or garden. Some of it can go into a holding tank for fish (see facing page).

Remove string algae from plant baskets and put them in the holding tank with the fish or in their own container with pond water.

Use a spray nozzle to blast debris from any stream and waterfall rocks; then spray the sides of the pool.

Rake up all debris from the bottom of the pond. Use a wet/dry vac to suck up the remaining muck left behind.

Backflush your biological filter following the manufacturer's directions. Clean all screens and filters on submersible pumps and clear out skimmer nets.

Begin refilling the pond; at the same time, drain some water out of the fish holding tank so you can add fresh water. This will help the fish adjust to the new pond water.

Add ocean salt to the fresh water in the pond, at the rate of 8 pounds per 1,000 gallons. The salt is beneficial to the fish, helps control freshwater parasites, and is a minor algicide.

Add a water conditioner (detoxifier) if your water contains chlorine or chloramine. Water conditioners also help the fish regain their protective slime coating after being disturbed.

Check that all the systems are working before returning your fish to the pond.

The filter and any screens should be lifted out and rinsed off monthly. When strip-cleaning the pond, give the filter and pump a thorough cleaning and check for wear.

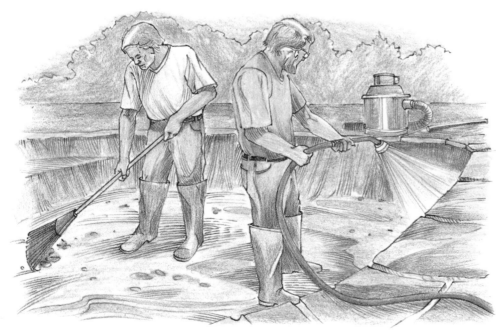

Cleaning a pond means removing all dead leaves and sunken debris yet not scrubbing away the thin layer of beneficial algae on the sides and bottom. A shop vacuum is useful for sucking up smaller material that the rake misses.

Maintaining Equipment

In areas where surface water routinely freezes, turn off the pumps during winter (when water temperatures approach 40°F/4°C). This won't harm a bio-logical filter, because its bacteria go dormant or die in cold water, anyway.

If your pond freezes in winter, external pumps, UV light water clarifiers, filters, and pipes or tubing not being used in winter must be drained to prevent water from freezing inside and breaking them. The submersible pump can be left in a pond, but be sure to clean the filter in the spring before starting it up again. If you remove a submersible pump from the pond, put it in a bucket of water until spring to keep the seals from drying out.

TROUBLESHOOTING PUMP PROBLEMS

Submersible pumps cannot be repaired as easily as other pumps, but their impeller assemblies (the shaft and propeller that move the water) can be checked and replaced if necessary. External pumps can be dismantled to replace broken or worn parts.

When water in a stream or waterfall is moving more slowly than is normal, the pump may be in trouble. First, check the pump's screen and filter. For a submersible pump, unplug the power cord and lift the pump to remove debris stuck in the screen. Some pumps have covers on the intake opening that can be removed for easier cleaning. If clogging is a regular problem, place the pump in a large bucket that has scores of holes drilled into it. The holes allow water to move freely, but keep the debris away from the pump screen.

For external pumps, shut off the power and clean out the leaf

SUBMERSIBLE PUMP ASSEMBLY

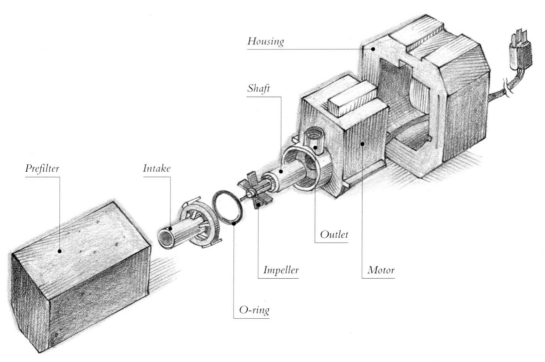

Housing
Shaft
Prefilter
Intake
Outlet
Impeller
Motor
O-ring

If your submersible pump malfunctions, you probably need a new one, unless the problem is the impeller assembly (shaft and impeller), which can be replaced. Often the entire pump is covered with a foam filter or a screen.

basket, which is designed to trap debris before it can go through the pump and possibly damage it. Both external and submersible pump motors can burn out if debris restricts water flow for an extended time.

PINPOINTING A LEAK

Whatever material your garden pond is made of, it may eventually tear or crack. The clue to a leak is a water level dropping faster than it normally would from evaporation. Fortunately, tears and cracks can be repaired. The trick is finding them.

Most leaks occur around a waterfall, in a streambed, or in seams where two pieces of flexible liner are joined. A sharp rock, toenail tears from a dog playing in the water, or the claws of a heron fishing in your pond can also cause leaks.

Before you start checking the pond itself, follow the routes of the water pipes to and from the pond to make sure that all connections are tight. The problem could simply be a leaking pipe or pipe connection.

Next, determine whether there really is a leak or if water from a stream or waterfall might be splashing out of the pool. Carefully check the streambed to see if leaves or small tree branches have become jammed against rocks and directed water away from its intended path. If you see a lot of splashed water around the waterfall, reduce the

External, or in-line, pumps normally have an attached leaf strainer to prevent debris from moving through the pump and damaging the impeller assembly. Remove the strainer, or leaf basket, from the container periodically, then clean and replace it.

rate of flow for 24 hours to see if the water level still drops.

Another way to check for a possible leak is to reroute the water through a large flexible hose so that it bypasses any streambed or waterfall. Mark the pond's water level at that time and leave the pump running for 24 hours. If the water level remains stable, the leak is in the stream or waterfall.

If none of the above is the problem, then you have to inspect the liner. If you have glued two pieces together (a practice most pool experts discourage), the leak is probably at this junction.

If you allow the water level to drop instead of refilling the pool, you'll eventually identify the level at which the leak is— wherever the water remains for several days. Then it's a matter of cleaning and carefully inspecting the liner just above the water line in hopes of finding the tear. (Occasionally, however, surrounding water-soaked ground may cause water to remain at a certain level even though the leak is below the water line.)

The worst-case scenario is that you cannot locate the leak and you simply have to remove the old liner and install a new one (see page 88–89).

PATCHING FLEXIBLE LINERS

Once a tear in a flexible liner is located, clean a 12-inch swath around the tear and let it dry.

For small holes, use a bicycle inner tube kit to make the repairs.

1 **For larger tears,** use EPDM repair tape. Pull off a length about 4 inches longer than the tear.

2 **Press the tape over the cut** by working from one end toward the other, to ensure that no bubbles are trapped under the tape.

3 **For added insurance,** cut another piece into narrow strips and press them over all the repair tape edges. (This same repair tape can be used on rigid-liner ponds with smooth surfaces.)

Repairs can also be made with special repair glue (available at your pond supply store) and a section of EPDM for patching. In this case, after you clean around the tear and let it dry, sand the surface lightly and clean again. Brush glue around the tear as wide as the patch is; then press the patch in place. Weigh the patch down for at least an hour.

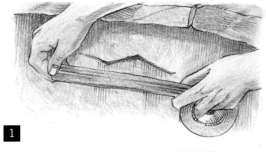

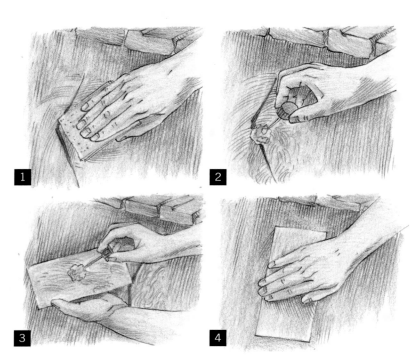

PATCHING RIGID LINERS

1 **To repair a rigid liner,** clean a 12-inch swath around the break, dry it, then roughen it with sandpaper. (If the liner is fiberglass, use a standard fiberglass repair kit.)

2 **Cut a patch** of 6-millimeter PVC sheeting to extend 6 inches beyond the tear. Apply PVC primer to the break so the glue will adhere better.

3 **Immediately brush the PVC** glue over the primer and over the patch itself. Press in place. Smooth out any bubbles.

4 **Hold the patch down firmly** for a few seconds while the glue sets.

REPAIRING CONCRETE POOLS

Concrete may crack if the ground under it settles. The preventive measure is to install the pond on undisturbed soil rather than fill dirt, and to ensure adequate reinforcement in the concrete.

1 **If a crack does develop,** drain the pond until the crack is fully exposed. Clean a wide swath around the crack and, using a hammer and cold chisel, chip out any loose material. Then use the chisel to undercut the sides of the crack slightly, the better to grip the patch.

2 **Apply a concrete bonding agent** in and around the crack; then use a caulking gun to inject concrete patching material purchased from a hardware or home supply store.

3 **Press the repair caulk** into the crack and smooth it with a wet finger. Scrape up any excess with a wide putty knife.

If you see numerous hairline cracks in the concrete, it's advisable to completely drain, clean, and then paint the pond. Once the pond is drained and all scum is scrubbed away, use a long-handled brush to scrub the surface with a mixture of 1 part muriatic acid to 2 parts water in a nonmetallic bucket. Always add the acid to the water, not the reverse. Wear gloves and eye protection during this cleaning process. When the concrete surface is dry, use a paint roller to apply an epoxy-based paint that will seal the hairline cracks. You can obtain these paints at swimming pool supply stores. Remember that because the concrete has been thoroughly cleaned, it will take some time to re-establish proper pH levels in the pond.

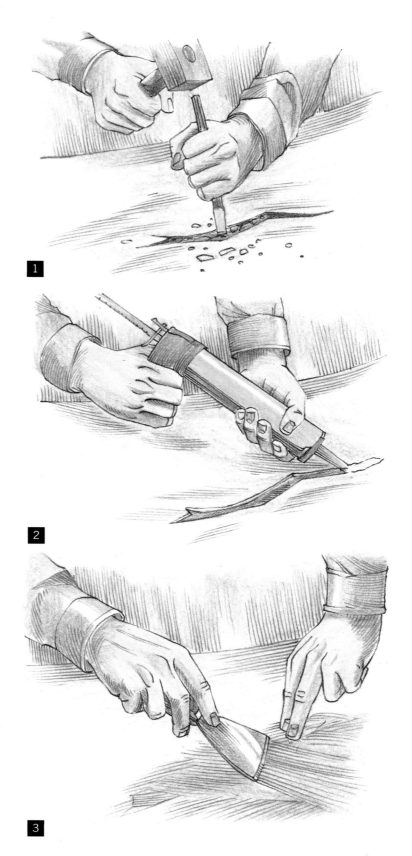

1

2

3

resources

SUPPLIERS

Aqua Art Pond
11-F Poco Way
American Canyon, CA 94503
707-642-7663
www.aquaart.com

Aquatic Eco-Systems, Inc.
1767 Benbow Court
Apopka, FL 32703
407-886-3939
www.aquaticeco.com

Fountain Builder
1841 County Road 977
Ignacio, CO 81137
970-883-5346
www.fountainbuilder.com

Lilypons Water Gardens
6400 Lilypons Road
Post Office Box 10
Buckeystown, MD 21717
800-999-5459
www.lilypons.com

**Maryland Aquatic
Nurseries**
3427 North Furnace Road
Jarrettsville, MD 21084
410-557-7615
www.marylandaquatic.com

Paradise Water Gardens
14 May Street
Whitman, MA 02382
800-955-0161
www.paradisewatergardens.com

Serenity Ponds and Streams
562-430-5284
www.serenityponds.com

Slocum Water Gardens
1101 Cypress Gardens
Boulevard
Winter Haven, FL 33884
863-293-7151
www.slocumwatergardens.com

Tetra Pond
3001 Commerce Street
Blacksburg, VA 24060
800-526-0650
www.tetra-fish.com

Van Ness Water Gardens
2460 North Euclid Avenue
Upland, CA 91784
800-205-2425
www.vnwg.com

Waterford Gardens
74 East Allendale Road
Saddle River, NJ 07458
210-327-0721
www.waterfordgardens.com

Wicklein's Water Gardens
1820 Cromwell Bridge Road
Baltimore, MD 21234
800-382-6716
www.wickleinaquatics.com

ORGANIZATIONS

**American Society of
Landscape Architects**
636 Eye St. NW
Washington, D.C. 20001-3736
202-898-2444
www.asla.org

**Associated Koi Clubs
of America**
www.akca.org

**International Water Lily and
Water Gardening Society**
6828 26th Street West
Bradentown, FL 34207
941-756-0880
www.iwgs.org

Mid-Atlantic Koi Club
www.makc.com

**Northwest Koi and Goldfish
Club**
10907 NE Morris Street
Portland, OR 97220
nwkg.tripod.com

**Washington Koi and Water
Garden Society**
10121 Evergreen Way
Everett, WA 98204
www.washingtonkoi.org

credits

PHOTOGRAPHERS

B = bottom; L = left; R = right;
T= top; M = middle (vertically);
C = center (horizontally)

Marion Brenner: 50; 65 T; 84; 86 T; 86 M; 86 B; 87 T; 87 B; 88 T; 88 M; 88 B; 89 T; 89 B; 98; 99 T; 99 B; 100 T; 100 B; 101 T; 101 B **Botanique Jardin de Montréal:** 141 TR; *Jean-Pierre Bellemare:* 139 BR; 143 BR; 144 TCL; *Normand Cornellier:* 150 TL; *Normand Fleury:* 147 TCL; *Romeo Meloche:* 139 TL; *Edith Morin:* 146 TC; *Michel Tremblay:* 2 **James Carrier:** 144 R **David Cavagnaro:** 146 BL; 149 BC **Crandall & Crandall:** 10 L; 17 T; 64 T; 149 TC; 154; 156; 166; 175 T **Robin B. Cushman:** 1; 4 T; 4 M; 6; 9 BR; 12 L; 12 BR; 14 R; 15 TL; 16 TR; 17 BL; 17 BR; 20; 24 BL; 26; 27 R; 30 B; 31; 33; 132; 146 TL; 148 TC; 152 TCL; 175 B; 191 **Alan & Linda Detrick:** 145 BL; 148 BC **Kerry A. Dressler:** 138 L; 139 MR; 140 ML; 142 TL; 142 BC; 142 BR; 143 BC; 144 L; 145 C; 149 TR; 151 TR; 152 TCR; 153 BCL **Scott Fitzgerrell:** 48 TR; 49 TL; 49 TL2; 49 TL3; 49 TC; 49 CM; 49 BMC **Roger Foley:** 4 B; 72 **Frank Gaglione:** 48 TC; 48 TC2; 48 TCR; 48 CM1; 48 CM2; 49 ML; 49 TR3; 49 BR; 61 R; 74 TL; 74 BL; 74 TR; 74 BR; 75 T; 75 TM; 75 BM; 75 B; 77 TL; 77 ML; 77 BL; 77 R; 78 T; 78 B; 79 T; 79 M; 79 B; 102; 103; 104 T; 104 B; 105 TR; 105 BR; 105 L; 106 T; 106 B; 107 T; 107 B; 108 T; 108 B; 109 L; 109 R; 110 T; 110 M; 110 B; 111 TR; 111 MR; 111 L **Steven Gunther:** 112 **Jamie Hadley:** 131 **Harry Haralambou:** 5 T; 9 BM; 18; 19; 22; 46; 59 T; 133 T; 133 B; 170; 172 B; 188 **Jerry Harpur:** 15 BL; 23 T; 29 B; 30 T; 116 R; 119; 121; 122; 124 TL; 140 TR; 151 TC; 165 **Marcus Harpur:** Front cover; 8 T; 29 T; 40; 42; 60 T; 63; 117; 118 B; 123 T; 145 TR; 149 BR **Philip Harvey:** 49 TR; 49 TR2 **Saxon Holt:** 23 B; 32; 34; 36; 80; 82 T; 82 B; 83 T; 83 B; 130 T; 135 L; 136 T; 143 BL; 146 TR; 147 BCR; 150 CR; 150 TR; 152 BCR; 153 CR; 167 T; 167 B; 172 T; 183 **Jean-Claude Hurni:** 5 M; 10 TR; 10 BR; 11 T; 12 TR; 28; 45; 64 MR; 64 B; 68; 114; 120 T; 124 BR; 126; 134; 135 M; 135 R; 138 T; 138 MR; 138 BR; 142 BL; 142 TC; 142 TR; 143 TL; 143 TC; 144 CR; 147 R; 148 R; 150 BL; 151 L; 151 BR; 152 L; 153 L; 153 TCL; 158 L; 159 L; 168 T; 168 B; 169; 173; 178 **Janet Loughrey:** 13 B; 16 L; 27 L; 39; 44; 116 L; 118 T; 123 MR; 123 BL; 123 BR; 136 B; 137; 145 TL; 148 L; 149 L; 150 BCL **Allan Mandell:** 8 BL; 15 TR; 124 MR; 130 B **Charles Mann:** 5 B; 11 B; 13 TR; 14 L; 16 BR; 24 T; 24 C; 70; 120 B; 150 BR; 159 R; 174; 176; 179 B; 180 **Sharron Milstein/Spindrift Photographics:** 181 **Norm Plate:** 56 TL; 56 TML; 56 BML; 56 BL; 57 (all 7); 59 B; 60 B; 61 L; 62; 179 T **Mark Rutherford:** 49 BCL; 49 BCR; 49 BL; 51 T; 51 B; 56 R **Perry D. Slocum:** 139 TR; 139 ML; 139 BL; 140 TL; 140 MR; 140 BR; 141 TL; 141 ML; 141 MR; 141 BL; 141 BR; 143 TR; 144 BCL; 146 BC; 147 L; 152 R; 158 R **Michael S. Thompson:** 65 B **Union Tools, Inc.:** 48 BCR; 48 BR; 48 BC; 48 TL; 48 BL **Paddy Wales:** 15 BR; 123 ML

ACKNOWLEDGMENTS

Special thanks go to Scott Soden of Artscapes in Belmont, California; Elaine Nobriga of Fountain Builder in Ignacio, Colorado; and Joel Head of Headwaters Landscaping in Santa Rosa, California, for their contributions to this book.

DESIGNERS

Jane Anders: 27 L **Art & Jardins, Inc.:** 28 **David Baird & Steve Taylor:** 9 BR; 31 **Robert Bateman:** 15 BR **Jinny Blom & HRH The Prince of Wales:** 118 B **Gerald Brazier:** 29 T **Anne Carton:** 30 T **Tom Chakas & Roger Raiche:** 130 B **Michael Charnaud:** 179 B **Beth Chatto:** 117; 124 TL **Linda Cochran:** 13 B **Daccord Landscape:** 114; 124 B **W & S Dixon:** 116 R **Paul Dyer:** 60 T **Glen Ellison:** 11 B **Embellissements paysagers Laval:** 11 T; 13 T; 178 **Rachel Foster:** 152 TCL **Kit & Fred Fulton:** 33 **Michael Glassman:** 154 **Joan Haldeman:** 156 **Marney Hall:** 23 T **Phil Hendrick:** 176 **Harold & Mary Hendrickson:** 26; 30 B **Jean-Claude Hurni & Milan Havlin:** 45 **Jean-Claude Hurni & Rêve-Rives:** 68 **Jim Kania:** 24 T **Tim Knapp:** 190 **La Casella, France:** 122 **Elizabeth Lair:** 15 TR **Alice Levien:** 59 T **Mary-Kate Mackey:** 175 B **Catharina Malmberg-Snodgrass et al:** 63 **Phyllis & Richard Null:** 6 **Marietta & Ernie O'Byrne:** 124 MR **Oehme & van Sweden Associates:** 15 BL; 29 B **Leann Olson:** 12 L **Jason Payne:** 8 T **Mr. & Mrs. J. Poulton:** 119 **Gary Ratway:** 147 BC **Sarah Ravens:** 40 **Lindsay Reaves:** 12 BR; 16 TR; 17 BL; 27 R **Ken Ruzicka:** 22; 133 T; 133 B; 170 **Kevin & Janet Square:** 132 **Brad Stangeland:** 14 R **David Stevens:** 42 **Troy Susan:** 8 BL **Philip Thornburg:** 118 T **Made Wijaya:** 165 **Nick Williams & Associates:** 17 T **Mike Zajic:** 36; 167 B

index

Page numbers in **boldface** refer to photographs.